BERNARD

of

CLAIRVAUX

BERNARD
of
CLAIRVAUX

A Lover Teaching the Way of Love

selected spiritual writings

introduced and edited by
M. Basil Pennington

New City Press

In homage and gratitude
Dom Bernardo Olivera, o.c.s.o.
Archabbot of Citeaux
Abbot General of the Cistercian Order of the Stricter Observance

Published in the United States by New City Press
202 Cardinal Rd., Hyde Park, NY 12538
©1997 New City Press

Cover design by Nick Cianfarani
Cover photo from Art Resource: Filippino Lippi (Florence, Italy)—The Apparition of the Madonna to Saint Bernard

Library of Congress Cataloging-in-Publication Data:

Bernard, of Clairvaux, Saint, 1090 or 91-1153
   [Selections. English. 1997]
   Bernard of Clairvaux, a lover teaching the way of love : selected spiritual writings / introduced and edited by M. Basil Pennington.
      p.   cm.
   Includes bibliographical references.
   ISBN 1-56548-089-9
   1. Spiritual life—Catholic Church. 2. Catholic Church--Doctrines. 3. Love—Religious aspects—Catholic Church.
   I. Pennington, M. Basil. II. Title.
   BX2179.B47E5   1996
   248—dc21   96-46247

1st printing: January 1997
2d printing: November 1997

Printed in the United States of America

Contents

Introduction

An awesome man

Any young man who can talk not only his older brothers but even his uncles into sending their wives off to nunneries in order to accompany him in entering a monastery really boggles the mind. What is the power of such a man? The young noble man, Bernard of Fontaines, better known to history as Bernard of Clairvaux, was twenty-one at the time he led thirty relatives to the gates of the new monastery at Citeaux. His magnetic charm did not abandon him as his life went on. So strong was it that when he preached at the University of Paris it is reported that more than half the student body left for the cloisters. This may be an exaggeration. It is a historical fact, however, that he did draw thousands into the cloister, that mothers hid their sons and wives their husbands when they heard Bernard was coming to town.

His power did not end there. Warring rulers were immediately reconciled when Bernard reached out to join their hands in peace. Vociferous heretics were struck dumb.

Cities were won over to a cause just by his presence. He was offered more than one miter and probably could have gone on to wear the papal tiara if he had not declined them and discretely put forward one of his spiritual sons. His was certainly the decisive voice in the healing of the papal schism of the 1130s, decisive in discerning who was the true heir of Peter.

That Bernard of Clairvaux was the father and leader of Christendom in the first half of the twelfth century is a historical fact. But it is not this almost frightening power that has endeared him to the centuries.

Nor is it his wonderful warm-hearted humanity. The letters he wrote bespeak a lover whose love reached out in all directions. He was not a man afraid of passion. Not a cleric fearful of women friends. Not a confident alien to the everyday concerns of family life. He was a loving father who knew disappointment and sore betrayal. There is nothing human that was alien to him. There is no human joy or sorrow that could not find a compassionate echo in his heart.

Oh, yes. He was human. He certainly learned some things the hard way. In his excessive zeal he almost destroyed his own health, not to say what he did to the men under him. But this was the young Bernard, who later demanded that his novices not overdo things and take good care of their health. He had a towering temper and he could rage. But he was always open to reconciliation. And when he was wrong, he readily ate humble porridge. He was a superior who knew how to say, "I'm sorry" to his subjects.

And he knew his share and more of ill health, a good bit undoubtedly brought on by pushing himself too far.

All of this does endear him to us. But still it is not what makes him present to the centuries. It is rather his spirituality: its total integrity and practicality, its depth and its sublimity, all exemplified in his own life, in his own spiritual journey, which is shared with us in his exceptionally beautiful writings.

Bernard's journey and ours

One thing we can be sure of. Though he entered the monastic way early enough, at least by our standards, before he knocked at the door of Citeaux, his chosen monastery, he had entered into a full classical education and mastered its arts. Unfortunately, the exquisite beauty of his carefully crafted Latin is largely lost in translation. Something of the poetry with its rich imagery gets through — for his prose was more poetic than the verse of many an acclaimed poet. Another thing is even more evident. As formed as he was in the schools, he was even more formed by what he aptly called the School of Love, the monastic way that used essentially one text: the sacred scriptures. One can easily believe that this man knew the whole of them by heart. Yet it was no mere rote knowledge. Inspired by the greatest Fathers of the Church, who were also his teachers, he plumbed their depths and brought forth rich meanings.

Bernard's skilled and powerful pen was used at times in service of his political and ecclesial ministries. And it was effective. But it was primarily in a spiritual ministry that he wrote, as a spiritual father. These are writings that come forth from the depths of his own being. They tell us of the journey he took. They show us the way. They invite us to follow. They promise the richest of rewards, rewards that respond to the deepest longings of our hearts, longings they invite us to uncover. Longings which we usually fear to uncover because we fear they can never be fulfilled. But Bernard assures us that they can be fulfilled. And he speaks not just to the chosen ones who live with him in the cloister. Nor does the assembly of the pious faithful define the limits of his audience. He dares to remind all of their sublime calling to the fullness of divine union.

> We have seen how every soul — even if burdened with sin, enmeshed in vice, ensnared by the allurements of pleasure, a captive in exile, imprisoned in the body, caught in mind, fixed in mire, bound to its members, a slave to care, distracted by business, afflicted with sorrow, wandering and straying, filled with anxious forebodings and uneasy suspicions, a stranger in a hostile land and, according to the prophet [Baruch], sharing the defilement of the dead and counted with those who go down under condemnation and without hope, has the power to turn and find it can not only breathe the fresh air of the hope of pardon and mercy, but can also dare to aspire to the nuptials of the Word, not fearing to enter into an alliance with God or to bear the sweet yoke of love with the King of angels. Why should it not venture with confidence into the presence of him by whose image it sees itself honored and in whose likeness it knows itself made glorious?

> (*Sermons on the Song of Songs* 83:1)

His writings reveal his journey

Saint Bernard's writings are for the most part what I would call occasional writings. They have been written for a specific occasion, usually at the request or urgent demand of a friend. Yet they do reveal where he himself is on the journey at the time of his writing. Undoubtedly, this monk with many connections, and the most celebrated writer of his times, received many requests. The ones he chose to respond to, sometimes very amply, would then most probably reflect what was uppermost in his own mind at the time. Thus it is that a survey of the spiritual writings that came from Bernard's pen during the course of his life enable us to follow his own journey into consummate holiness.

His first work is especially revealing. Still free from the demands that reputation and popularity would put upon him, he could write at leisure on that which was closest to his heart and most fundamental in his thinking. He chose to write about the event that crowns our race and was the most significant moment in its history: the annunciation and incarnation, the visit of the angel Gabriel to the Virgin Mary. It was the moment when God himself became one with us in our humanity as he was conceived in the womb of the Virgin. The persons of Jesus and Mary were central to Bernard's life ever since a boyhood vision on the night of Christmas. There he saw the wonder of God become man and coming forth from the Virgin. In his four *Homilies in Praise of the Virgin Mother*, he brings us through that dramatic moment with moving drama. The fact that God became one with us in our humanity, suffered, died, rose and ascended *for us* is the source of our faith, the cause of our hope, the reality that calls forth all our love.

Bernard's pen sings rapturously of this Woman, so favored by God, chosen dwelling place of the divine. It was a theme his pen would return to more than once as the years went by. For Mary was to him more than the mother he received at the foot of the cross in the person of the disciple whom Jesus loved. She was his advocate, his life, his sweetness, his hope; she was the prototype of the Church, the mystic spouse of his Beloved.

She was the one closest, dearest, most precious to his Jesus. And Jesus was his all. His pen would write with rapturous beauty of this most holy name. He would celebrate as no other the nuptials of the soul, his soul, with this divine bridegroom. He would also dip his pen in the blood and write of the Beloved's most bitter passion. And most bitter of all, but also most loving, he would accept that Jesus had in some way to go away so that the Spirit, the very kiss of God, could come.

So, as Bernard set out on the journey, Jesus and Mary were very present to him. And his way was clear. In response to a clear vocation, he had embraced the Cistercian way of life, a life bent on living the gospel in its fullness as it was laid out in Benedict of Nursia's *Rule for Monasteries*. Central to Benedict's spiritual program, a school of the Lord's service, is humility. He constructs a twelve-rung ladder of humility, that in essence sums up the whole of his spiritual teaching. With self-deprecating humor Bernard pointed out that one could go down a ladder as well as up, and that he was more familiar with tumbling down what had become steps of pride. He went on to describe them with great insight, without ever abandoning his sense of humor.

But far more important, he pointed out that we do not need a ladder unless we want to ascend to something. Where do we want to go? Humility is truth. We want to ascend the steps of truth. When we truly know ourselves in humility, then we know our fellows in compassion, and we are ready to come to know God in contemplation. Truth in action is love. The steps of love are just another way of expressing the same journey into God, into communion and union.

Bernard's is the way of love. With the Cistercians, largely under his leadership, Benedict's school of the Lord's service was transformed into a *scola caritatis*, a school of love. Bernard's little treatise *On Loving God* is but the springboard for what would become his life-long exploration of love in commenting on sacred scripture's great love song, *The Song of Songs*.

But before embarking on this, Bernard stopped to explore who is the lover and how does he love, where does his power of love come from. As he wrote in his treatise, "It is impossible for a person by his own power of free will to turn wholly to the will of God and not rather to his or her own will." Love is the freest of things; it can never be forced. Yet the Lord says, "Without me you can do nothing." How does God work in us by his grace so that at the same time we remain truly free to love him freely? This is the question Bernard explores in the little work he wrote for his friend, William of Saint Thierry: *Grace and Free Choice*.

One of the beautiful things about Bernard's journey is the friendship he enjoyed with William of Saint Thierry. From the day William first laid eyes on Bernard, he loved him deeply and wanted to be with him. But Bernard fully respected William's own vocation and insisted his friend continue to pursue it. However, when he was sick for a long period and confined to the infirmary, he did allow for his friend who was also sick to be brought to share his confinement. Laying side by side they spoke for weeks of the Song of Songs. From then on the friends' journey was similar. While Bernard wrote *On Loving God*, William wrote *On the Nature and Dignity of Love*. William was working on his *Commentary on Romans* when he called forth Bernard's essay on *Grace and Free Choice*. Together they went ahead to explore the Song of Songs, Bernard writing his *Sermons* and William his *Commentary*. And it was William who called for an interruption on the part of both of them for the more painful business of responding to the dangers arising from the overly rationalistic theology of Peter Abelard. It would be difficult to overestimate the significance of this friendship in the life of both of these men, especially given the passionate expressions we find in Bernard's letters to William. Even a man as extraordinarily endowed as Bernard of Clairvaux needed someone to walk with him on the journey, someone to support and challenge him, to call him forth. As Bernard wrote to another: "The man who is his own master is the disciple of a fool."

As the years unfolded, Bernard was involved in many of the cares of the Church. These called forth various writings. And his long series of *Sermons on the Song of Songs* addresses many of these cares. We also find in these sermons some very personal sharing. Undoubtedly the most touching is the beautiful eulogy for his brother Gerard. His humble recital of his altercation with his brother Bartholomew reveals another side of him. But essentially the *Sermons on the Song of Songs* is an ample presentation, very rich with poetic imagery, of the way of asceticism and prayer that leads to the fullest mystical experience. The fact that it is interwoven with so much of the stuff of life was not unintended. In doing this Bernard tells us in a very concrete and effective way that the spiritual journey, even the journey in the highest realms of mystical experience, takes place in the course of everyday life. Even as we truly seek God and seek to develop a life of prayer, we still have to live our life as it unfolds under the loving care of divine providence. It is one life, all woven together, even though it is sometimes difficult for us to see how this is so. But the increasing presence of the Holy Spirit in our lives brings us to the understanding of this through his gifts.

I invite you now to journey with Bernard of Clairvaux, saint and abbot, a true spiritual father. Let him be present to you as you listen to him speaking through these words he himself wrote precisely for our guidance. Don't just read these texts but listen to them, enter into conversation with them — with him. Let the centrality of the incarnation, the presence of Jesus and his Mother Mary, be renewed in your life. Gain insight into the pride that keeps you from ascending the ladder of truth and love. Know yourself as a truly free person who has but to ascent to the loving activity of God in your life. Find not only the true freedom of the child of God but the unbelievable intimacy of a lover brought into the inner life of the Trinity.

Translations

The translations used here are taken for the most part from *The Works of Bernard of Clairvaux*, published by Cistercian Publications in their Cistercian Fathers Series. However, I have not hesitated to revise them when I felt Bernard's eloquent Latin could be better expressed. I am grateful to all the translators and editors of Cistercian Publications, who have been working with me these past twenty-five years to make the extensive corpus of Bernardine writings available in English. The labor is far from finished. But it is my hope that this brief anthology will not only help you greatly on your own spiritual journey but also invite you to drink more deeply of the wisdom of this great spiritual father in the many volumes of his writings already published. A list of the published works, as well as other studies that might be helpful, will be found at the end of this volume along with a brief chronology of Bernard's life.

M. Basil Pennington, o.c.s.o

An Incarnational Spirituality

When Bernard was still a young spiritual father, in his late twenties and early thirties, and his renown had not yet brought to his door the demands of the many, he enjoyed a certain amount of holy leisure. This was especially true during the periods when illness set him apart from the community and the regular exercises of the monastic life. It was during this period that he first took up his pen to begin what was going to be a very productive literary career, sharing with a wider audience his rich spiritual teaching.

His first work, *Homilies in Praise of the Virgin Mother*, four sermons on the gospel of the annunciation, makes two things clear to us with its opening lines. Although much of Bernard's writing took the form of homilies and sermons, this is only a literary form; the products do not necessarily represent anything ever preached, though undoubtedly the content did find its way into the many sermons he did preach. Secondly, we are immediately put in touch with Bernard's tremendous love for and appreciation of the sacred scriptures, which will ever remain his primary source and inspiration.

This work of devotion also puts us in touch with what was the foundation and center of Bernard's spiritual life: the incarnation, God become man, the man Jesus Christ, who is a God who so loves us that he comes to dwell among us to share our humanity, to make it possible for us to share his divinity. This naturally and immediately leads to a beautiful and tender devotion not only to the God-man but also to his mother, the woman the Incarnate loved above all and associated so intimately with himself in his saving mission of love. Bernard's prose turns to poetry here. And it has its drama also. It is rich in its sensuous image. This very warm, affective devotion would ever remain a part of Bernard's spirituality. We shall share further on some of his later expressions of it in passages from, among other sources, his *Sermons on the Song of Songs* and his treatise *On Loving God*. Also worthy of note here is Bernard's emphasis on that foundational virtue: humility. It would be the subject of his next literary production, the first steps on the journey to divine union, which we shall see in the next section.

The Beginning — God Becomes Man

The Angel Gabriel was sent by God to a city of Galilee named Nazareth, to a virgin engaged to a man whose name was Joseph, of the House of David, and the virgin's name was Mary. And so on.

We may wonder what the evangelist's intention was when he made such specific mention of so many proper names. I think he wanted to be sure we would not give careless hearing to what he was going to narrate so carefully. You notice that he mentions the messenger who was sent, the Lord by whom he was sent, the virgin to whom he was sent, and the virgin's fiancé. He even mentions by name their race, the city they came from, and the district.

Why? Do you suppose that any of these details were set down without a good reason? Of course not! If no leaf can fall from a tree without cause, and not a single sparrow falls to the ground without the heavenly Father's knowledge, am I to think that a superfluous word could fall from the lips of the holy evangelist — especially in recording the sacred history of the Word? I think not. All his words contain supernatural mysteries and are full of heavenly sweetness, if only they have a diligent reader (one who knows how to suck honey out of the rock, and oil out of the hardest stone). Now in those days the mountains dripped with sweet wine and the hills flowed with milk and honey. Then the heavens dropped dew from above and the clouds showered the Just One, causing the earth to open out and, rejoicing, to blossom with the Savior. The Lord showed his kindness and our earth bore its fruit. On the mountain of mountains, the mountain rich and fat, mercy and truth met, justice and peace kissed. Then, too, the holy evangelist, himself one of the mountains — and by no means the least — made known to us in words flowing like honey the beginning of our salvation, so long desired. It was as if a gentle southerly wind were blowing, as if the Sun of righteousness were shining close by, causing sweet smelling spiritual spices to flow. Yes, and now may God send forth his Word and may it make them flow in us. If only his Spirit would inspire us that we might understand the gospel words. If only they could become for our hearts more desirable than gold, than the most precious stone, and sweeter than honey and the honeycomb.

The evangelist writes: "The angel Gabriel was sent by God." I do not think that Gabriel was one of the lesser angels, one of those ambassadors usually sent to earth to handle affairs. I deduce this from his name, which means "God's fortitude."

"The angel Gabriel was sent by God." Where? "To a city of Galilee named Nazareth." Like Nathaniel, we might well wonder whether anything good can come from Nazareth. Nazareth means flower. It seems to me that the heavenly promises, which were made to the patriarchs Abraham, Isaac and Jacob, were some sort of seed of divine knowledge cast down, so to speak, from heaven to earth. They are the seed of which it is written: "If the Lord God of hosts had not left us a seed, we should have been like Sodom and reduced like Gomorrah." This seed flowered first in the wonderful doings which were shown forth in symbols and in riddles as Israel came out of Egypt, all along the way through the desert to the Land of Promise, and afterward in the visions and foretellings of the prophets, in the setting up of the kingdom and the priesthood, even until Christ's coming. Not without reason do we understand Christ to be the fruit of the flowers sprung from this seed, for David says, "The Lord will look with kindness upon the earth and it shall bear fruit." And again, "I will place the fruit of your womb upon your throne." It was at Nazareth, therefore, that Christ's birth was first announced, because in the flower lies the hope of fruit to come.

Into that particular city, then, the angel Gabriel was sent by God. To whom? "To a virgin engaged to a man whose name was Joseph." Who is this virgin noble enough to be greeted by an angel and yet humble enough to be the fiancé of a workman?

How gracious is this union of virginity and humility! A soul in whom humility embellishes virginity and virginity ennobles humility finds no little favor with God. Imagine then how much more worthy of reverence must she have been whose humility was raised by motherhood and whose virginity consecrated by her childbearing. You are told that she is a virgin. You are told that she is humble. If you are not able to imitate the virginity of this humble maid, then imitate the humility of the virgin maid. Virginity is a praiseworthy virtue, but humility is by far the more necessary. The one is only counseled, the other is demanded. To the first you have been invited, to the second you are obliged. Concerning the first he said: "He who is able to receive this, let him receive it." Of the second it is said, "Truly I say to you, unless you become like this little child, you will not enter the kingdom of heaven." The first is rewarded, the second is required. You can be saved without virginity, without humility you cannot be. Humility which deplores the loss of virginity can still find favor. Yet I dare say that without humility not even Mary's virginity would have been acceptable. The Lord says, "Upon whom shall my Spirit rest, if not upon the one that is humble and contrite in spirit?" *On the humble*, he says, not *on the virgin*. Had Mary not been humble, then the Holy Spirit would not have rested upon her. Had the Holy Spirit not rested upon her, Mary would not have become pregnant. How indeed could she have conceived by the Holy Spirit without the Holy Spirit? It seems evident then that she conceived by the Holy Spirit because, as she herself said, God "regarded the humility of his handmaiden" rather than her virginity. And even if it was because of her virginity that she found favor, she conceived nevertheless on account of her humility. Thus there is no doubt that her virginity was found pleasing because her humility made it so.

(*Homilies in Praise of the Blessed Virgin Mary* 1:1ff)

But in Mary there is something else still more admirable: her childbearing allied with her virginity. Never since the world began had it been known for any woman to be at once a mother and a virgin. If you just think whose mother she is, surely you must be astounded at such marvelous greatness. Who could ever admire this enough? To your way of thinking, or rather, not to yours but Truth's, should she not be exalted above all the choirs of angels, she who bore God the Son? Who else would dare, as Mary did, to call the Lord and God of angels her son, saying, "Son, why have you treated us so?" Would any angel dare this? They already consider it a great favor to be made and to be called angels by grace, when by nature they are no more than spirits, as David witnesses when he says, "He makes the spirits his angels." Yet the same majesty whom they served with awe and reverence Mary, knowing herself the mother, confidently called her son. Nor did God disdain to be called what he had deigned to become. As the evangelist tells us a bit later, "He was obedient to them." Who? God. To whom? To humans. God, I repeat, to whom the angels are subject, he whom the principalities and the powers obey, was obedient to Mary. And not only to Mary but to Joseph, too, for Mary's sake. Marvel then at these two things: the gracious kindness of the Son and the surpassing dignity of the mother. Choose which you consider more wonderful. Just imagine! Double marvel! God does what a woman says — unheard-of humility. A woman outranks God — unparalleled sublimity.

(Homilies in Praise of the Blessed Virgin Mary 1:7)

This is what the evangelist is telling us here when he states that an angel was sent by God to a virgin. He says *by God to a virgin*: from the highest to the humble, from the Maker to the handmaiden, from the Creator to the creature! How kind God is! How matchless is the Virgin! Behold, God has sent down for the Virgin. Behold, Mary is being spoken for by the angel. Put your ear to the door, strain to listen to the tidings he brings. Maybe you will hear soothing words to comfort you.

(Homilies in Praise of the Blessed Virgin Mary 2:2)

Let us now hear what the angel thinks about this child to whom even before conception he has given so great a name. The angel says, "He will be great and will be called the Son of the Most High." Is he not great when there is no end of his greatness? And he says, "Who is great like our God?" He is clearly great, he is as great as the Most High, for he is himself none other than the Most High. Nor, being the Son of the Most High, did he count it robbery to be equal to the Most High. The one who must be thought to have premeditated robbery is he who having been called out of nothing into the form of an angel, likened himself to his Maker and snatched at what belongs to the Son of the Most High, to him who in the form of God was not made by God but begotten. The Most High Father, although he is almighty, could neither fashion a creature equal to himself nor beget a Son unequal to himself. He made the angel very great but not as great as himself and therefore not most high. That the only-begotten Son, whom he did not make but begot, the Almighty from the Almighty, the Most High from the Most High, co-eternal with the eternal, claimed to be compared to him in every way, he thought neither robbery nor effrontery. How rightly then will he be called great: He is the Son of the Most High.

But why does the angel say, "He will be," and not, "He is" great? His greatness, forever unvarying, is not subject to growth. He will not be greater after his conception than before. Is it possible the angel meant to say that he who is a great God will become a great man? In that case he was right to say, "He will be great." For he will be a great man, a great teacher, a great prophet. We do in fact read of him in the gospel, "A great prophet has risen up among us." In the past there were lesser prophets who foretold the coming of this great prophet: "Behold, a great prophet shall come and he shall restore Jerusalem." You, however, virgin maid, will give birth to a little child, you will feed a little child and suckle a little one. But as you gaze at this little one, think how great he is. He will indeed be great, for God will magnify him in the sight of kings, and all kings will come to adore him, all nations shall serve him. So let your soul magnify the Lord, for he will be great and will be called Son of the Most High. He will be great and he who is mighty will do great things in you. Holy is his name. What holier name could he have than to be called the Son of the Most

High? May this great Lord be magnified by us little ones as well. That he might make us great, he was made a little child. "Unto us a child is born," someone said, "for us a son is given." For us, I repeat, not for himself. He who was born of the Father before all ages was of more noble birth and had no need to be born in time from a mother. And he was not even born for the angels. They had him great among them and had no need of a little child. He was born for us, therefore, and given to us because we need him.

Now that he has been born and given to us, let us accomplish the purpose of this birth and this donation. He came for our good, let us use him to our good. Let us work out our salvation from the Savior. Look, a little child is put in our midst.

O little child, so desired by your children! You are indeed a little child but a child in evil-doing, not a child in wisdom. Let us make every effort to become like this little child. Because he is meek and humble of heart, let us learn from him, lest he who is great, even God, should have been made a little one for nothing, lest he should have died to no purpose and have been crucified in vain. Let us learn his humility, imitate his gentleness, embrace his love, share his suffering, be washed in his blood. Let us offer him the propitiation for our sins, because for this he was born and given to us. Let us offer him up in the sight of the Father, offer him too in his own sight, for the Father did not spare his own Son but gave him up for us all. And the Son emptied himself, taking the form of a servant. He freely poured out his soul in death and was numbered with brigands. He bore the sins of many and interceded for transgressors that they might not perish. How can they perish who the Son prayed might not perish, and for whose life the Father gave up his Son to death? We may therefore hope for forgiveness equally from them both, for they are equally merciful in their steadfast love, united in a single powerful will, one in the substance of the Godhead in which together with the Holy Spirit they live and reign, God, through all the ages of ages. Amen.

(Homilies in Praise of the Blessed Virgin Mary 3:12ff)

Then the angel said, "The Holy Spirit will come upon you and the power of the Most High will overshadow you." What does "and the power of the Most High will overshadow you" mean? "Let him who can grasp this, grasp it." Who indeed can, except perhaps she who alone deserved to have this most blessed experience. Who can grasp by his or her intelligence and discern with reason not only the way in which the inaccessible Splendor could pour himself out into a virginal womb, but also how, in order that she might support the approach of the Inaccessible, it became a shade for the rest of this body, a small portion of which he had vivified and appropriated? And perhaps it was for this reason the angel used the words, "He will overshadow you." Because the event was so great a mystery that the Trinity wished to accomplish it in the Virgin alone and with her alone, and she alone was allowed to understand it because she alone was allowed to experience it. Let us admit then that "the Holy Spirit will come upon you" means "You will become pregnant by his power." And the words, "The power of the Most High shall overshadow you" mean "The means by which you are to conceive by the Holy Spirit is that the Power of God and the Wisdom of God, Christ, will be so concealed and so hidden in the shadowing of his most secret counsel that it shall be known only to him and to you." It is as if the angel replied to the Virgin, "Why ask me about something which you are going soon to experience in yourself? You will find out, how happily you will find out, and your teacher will be none other than he who works this.

I have been sent only to announce this virginal conception, not to bring it about. This is something which can only be taught by the giver and learnt only by the receiver. 'Therefore the Holy to be born of you will be called the Son of God.' This means you are to conceive, but by the Holy Spirit, not by a man. You will, therefore, conceive the Power of the Most High, the Son of God. 'Therefore the Holy to be born of you will be called the Son of God.' This means he who comes from the bosom of the Father into your womb will not only overshadow you. He will even take to himself something of your substance. He who is already the Son of God, begotten of the Father before all ages, will henceforth be acknowledged to be your son as well. In this way, the Son born of God will be yours, and the child born of you will be God's, in such a way that there will be not two sons but only one. Although he had one thing from you and another from the Father, yet you will not each have your own son, but he will be the one Son of both of you."

(Homilies in Praise of the Blessed Virgin Mary 4)

Virgin, you have heard what will happen, you have heard how it will happen. You have a double reason for astonishment and rejoicing. Rejoice, O Daughter of Sion, and be exceedingly glad, Daughter of Jerusalem. And since you have heard joyous and glad tidings, let us hear that joyous reply we long for, so that broken bones may rejoice. You have heard what is to happen, I say, and you have believed. Believe also the way you have heard it is to happen. You have heard that you will conceive and bear a son. You have heard that it will be by the Holy Spirit and not by a man. The angel is waiting for your reply. It is time for him to return to the One who sent him.

We, too, are waiting for this merciful word, my Lady, we who are miserably weighed down under a sentence of condemnation. The price of our salvation is being offered to you. If you consent, we shall immediately be set free. We all have been made in the eternal Word of God, and look, we are dying. In your brief reply we shall be restored and be brought back to life. Doleful Adam and his unhappy offspring, exiled from paradise, implore you, kind Virgin, to give this answer. David asks it. Abraham asks it. All the other holy patriarchs, your very own fathers, beg it of you, as do those now dwelling in the region of the shadow of death. For it the whole world is waiting, bowed down at your feet. And rightly, too, because on your answer depends the comfort of the afflicted, the redemption of captives, the deliverance of the damned, the salvation of all the sons and daughters of Adam, your whole race. Give your answer quickly, my Virgin. My Lady, say this word which earth and hell and heaven itself are waiting for. The very King and Lord of all, he who has so desired your beauty, is eager for your answer and assent, by which he proposes to save the world. Him whom you pleased by your silence, you will now please even more by your word. He calls out to you from heaven, "O beautiful among women, let me hear your voice." If you let him hear your voice, then he will let you see our salvation. Is not this what you have been waiting for, what you have been weeping for and sighing after day and night in your prayers? What then? Are you the one who was promised or must we look for another? No. It is you and no one else. You, I say, are the one we were promised, you are the one we are expecting, you are the one we have longed for, in whom your holy ancestor Jacob, as he was approaching death, put all his hope of eternal life, saying, "I shall wait for your salvation, Lord." You are she in whom and by whom God, our king himself, before all ages decided to work out our salvation in the midst of the earth. Why hope from another for what is now being offered to you? Why expect from another woman what will soon be shown forth through you? If you will only consent and say the word. So answer the angel quickly, or rather, through the angel answer God. Only say the word and receive the Word. Give yours and conceive God's. Breathe one fleeting word and embrace the everlasting Word. Why do you delay? Why be afraid? Believe, give praise and receive. Let humility take courage and shyness confidence. This is not the moment for virginal simplicity to forget prudence. In this circumstance alone, O prudent Virgin, do not fear presumption, for if your reserve pleased by its silence how much more must your goodness speak. Blessed Virgin, open your heart to faith, your lips to consent, and your womb to your Creator. Behold, the long-desired of all nations is standing at the door and is knocking. Oh, what if he should pass by because of your delay and, sorrowing, you should again have to seek him whom your soul loves? Get up, run, open! Get up by faith, run by prayer, open by consent!

"Behold," she says, "I am the handmaiden of the Lord. Let it be done unto me according to your word."

(*Homilies in Praise of the Blessed Virgin Mary* 4:8f)

Let it be to me concerning the Word according to your word. May the Word, who in the beginning was with God, become flesh of my flesh, according to your word. I beg that the Word be to me not a word which once pronounced fades away, but the Word which conceived remains, clothed with flesh and not with air. Let it be to me a Word not audible to the ear but visible to the eyes, one which hands can touch and arms can carry. Let it be to me not a written and mute word, but one incarnate and living, that is to say, not one scratched by dumb signs on dead skins but one in human form truly given, lively, within my chaste womb, not the tracings of a dead pen but the working of the Holy Spirit.

Let it be to me as it has never been to any person before me and will be to no one after me. For in many and various ways God has spoken of old to our fathers by the prophets. And it is known that the word of the Lord was put into the ear of some, into the mouth of others, and even into the hands of a few. But I ask that it be to me in my womb according to your word. I do not want it to be a word proclaimed to me in discourse, symbolized in figure, or dreamed in the imagination. But one silently breathed forth into my being, personally incarnate, corporally present in my womb. May the Word which could not and had no need to be made in himself, deign to be in me, deign to be done unto me according to your word. Let it be done for the whole world, but let it be done unto me uniquely, according to your word.

(*Homilies in Praise of the Blessed Virgin Mary* 4:11)

Jesus, the Incarnate Word

Our Savior is a faithful counselor who can never deceive us or be deceived. He is a strong helper whom labor never wearies. He is a mighty protector who will quickly enable us to trample underfoot the powers of Satan. For he is the wisdom of God who is ever ready to instruct the ignorant, the power of God for whom it is so easy to strengthen the weak and rescue those in danger. Therefore, my brothers and sisters, in all our doubts and perplexities let us have recourse to so wise a master. In all our undertakings let us invoke the assistance of so powerful a helper. In our every combat let us commit our souls to the keeping of so faithful a protector. He has come into the world so that living here in us, with us, and for us he might illumine our darkness, lighten our labors, and guard us from all dangers.

(*Seventh Sermon for Advent*)

Do we feel sad? Let the name of Jesus come into our heart, from there let it spring to our mouth, so that shining like the dawn it may dispel all darkness and make a cloudless sky. Do we fall into sin? Does despair even urge us to suicide? Let us but invoke this life-giving name and our will to live will be at once renewed. The hardness of heart that is our common experience, the apathy bred of indolence, bitterness of mind, repugnance for the things of the spirit — have they ever failed to yield in presence of this saving name? The tears dammed up by the barrier of our pride — how have they not burst forth again with sweeter abundance at the thought of Jesus' name? And where is the one who, terrified and trembling before impending peril, has not been suddenly filled with courage and rid of fear by calling on the strength of the name? Where is the one who, tossed on the rolling waves of doubt, did not quickly find certitude by recourse to the clarity of Jesus' name? Was ever a person so discouraged, so beaten down by affliction, to whom the sound of this name did not bring new resolve? In short, for all the ills and disorders to which flesh is heir this name is medicine. For proof we have no less than his own promise, "Call upon me in the day of trouble. I will deliver you, and you shall glorify me." Nothing so curbs the onset of anger, so allays the upsurge of pride. It cures the wound of envy, controls unbridled extravagances and quashes the flame of lust. It cools the thirst of covetousness and banishes the itch of unclean desire. For when I name Jesus I set before me a man who is meek and humble of heart, kind, prudent, chaste, merciful, flawlessly upright and holy in the eyes of all. And this same man is the all-powerful God whose way of life heals me, whose support is my strength. All these re-echo for me at the hearing of Jesus' name.

(On the Song of Songs, 15:6)

What have you to do with righteousness if you are ignorant of Christ, who is the righteousness of God? Where, I ask, is true prudence, except in the teaching of Christ? Or true justice, if not from Christ's mercy? Or true temperance, if not in Christ's life? Or true fortitude, if not in Christ's passion? Only those can be called prudent who are imbued with his teaching. Only those are just who have had their sins pardoned through his mercy. Only those are temperate who take pains to follow his way of life. Only those are courageous who hold fast to the example of his patience when buffeted by suffering. Vainly therefore will anyone strive to acquire the virtues if he or she thinks they may be obtained from any source other than the Lord of virtues whose teaching is the seed-bed of prudence, whose mercy is the well-spring of justice, whose life is a mirror of temperance, whose death is the badge of fortitude.

(On the Song of Songs, 22:11)

The faithful know how totally they need Jesus and him crucified. While they admire and embrace in him that charity which surpasses all knowledge, they are ashamed at failing to give what little they have in return for so great a love and honor. Easily they love more who realize they are loved more: "He loves less to whom less is given." . . . The Church sees King Solomon with the diadem his mother had placed on his head. She sees the Father's only Son carrying his cross, the Lord of majesty slapped and covered with spittle. She sees the Author of life and glory pierced by nails, wounded by a lance, saturated with abuse, and finally laying down his precious life for his friends. She beholds this, and the sword of love all the more pierces through her soul, and she cries: "Cushion me with flowers, pile up apples around me, for I languish with love."

These apples are certainly the pomegranates the bride introduced into her Beloved's garden. Picked from the tree of life, they had changed their natural taste for that of the heavenly bread, their color for that of Christ's blood. At last she sees death dead and death's author defeated. She beholds captivity led captive from hell to earth and from earth to heaven so that in the name of Jesus every knee bends in heaven, on earth and in hell. She beholds the earth, which produced thorns and thistles under the ancient curse, blooming again by the grace of a new blessing. And in all this she thinks of the psalm which says: "And my flesh flourishes again, with all my will I shall praise him." She wishes to add to the fruits of the passion which she had picked from the tree of the cross some of the flowers of the resurrection whose fragrance will induce the Bridegroom to visit her more often.

Then she says: "You are fair my Beloved and handsome, our couch is strewn with flowers." By the couch she reveals clearly enough what she desires, and by declaring that it is strewn with flowers she indicates clearly whence she hopes to obtain what she wants: not by her own merits but with flowers picked in the field the Lord has blessed. Christ loved flowers. He willed to be conceived and raised in Nazareth. The heavenly Bridegroom enjoys those perfumes so much that he willingly and often enters the chambers of the heart he finds decked with these flowers and fruits. Where he sees a mind constantly occupied with the grace of the passion and the glory of the resurrection, there he is constantly and willingly present.

If we wish to have Christ for a guest often, we must keep our hearts fortified by the testimony of our faith in the mercy of him who died for us, and in the power of him who rose from the dead. As David said: "These two things I have heard: Power belongs to God and mercy to you, O Lord." The testimonies of both these are ever so believable. Christ died for our sins and rose again from the dead for our justification. He ascended to heaven for our protection, sent the Spirit for our consolation, and will someday return for our fulfillment. He certainly showed his mercy in dying, his power in rising again, and both of these in all the other things he did for us.

(*On Loving God* 7ff)

Afterward Jesus showed them a higher degree of love when he said, "It is the Spirit who gives life, the flesh profits nothing." I think Paul had reached this level when he said, "Even if we once knew Christ in the flesh, we know him thus no longer." Perhaps this was also true of the prophet [Jeremiah] who said, "A Spirit before our face is Christ the Lord." When he adds, "Under his shadow we will live among the heathens," he seems to me to speak on behalf of the beginners, in order that they may at least rest in the shade, since they know they are not strong enough to bear the heat of the sun. They may be nourished by the sweetness of his humanity, since they are not yet able to perceive the things which are of the Spirit of God. The shade of Christ, I suggest, is the flesh which overshadowed Mary and tempered for her the bright splendor of the Spirit. Therefore, in this human devotion there is in the meantime consolation for who does not as yet have the Spirit who gives life, at least not in the same way as those who say, "A Spirit before our face is Christ the Lord." And again, "If we once knew Christ in the flesh, we know him thus no longer." For there is no love of Christ at all without the Holy Spirit, even if this here is in the flesh and without its fullness. The measure of such love is this: Its sweetness seizes the whole heart and draws it completely from the love of all flesh and every sensual pleasure. Really, this is what it means to love with the whole heart. If I prefer to the humanity of my Lord someone joined to me by ties of blood or some sensual pleasure, it obviously proves that I do not love with my whole heart. Because it is divided between its own interests and the love of the One who taught me as a man, both by his words and examples. Would I not seem to give my love partly to him and partly to my own? As he once said, "Whoever loves father or mother more than me is not worthy of me, and whoever loves son or daughter more than me is not worthy of me." To put it briefly, to love with one's whole heart means to put the love of his sacred humanity before everything that tempts us from within or without. Among these temptations we must also count the glory of the world, because its glory is that of the flesh, and those who delight in it without a doubt are persons of the flesh.

Of course, this devotion to the humanity of Christ is a gift, a great gift of the Spirit. I have called it carnal with comparison to that other love which does not know the Word as flesh as much as it knows the Word as wisdom, justice, truth, holiness, loyalty, strength, and whatever else could be said in this manner. Christ is truly all these things. "He became for us the wisdom of God, and justice, and sanctification and redemption."

 Take as an example two persons: One of them feels a share in Christ's sufferings, is affected and easily moved at the thought of all that Christ suffered. This person is nourished and strengthened by the sweetness of this devotion to good and honest and worthy actions. But the other person is always aflame with zeal for justice, eager for the truth and for wisdom. Her life, her habits are saintly, ashamed of boasting, avoiding criticism, never knowing envy, hating pride. She not only flees all human glory but shrinks from it and avoids it, every strain of impurity both in body and soul she loathes and eradicates. Finally, she spurns every evil as if naturally, and embraces what is good. If you would compare the feelings of these two, would it not appear that the latter was superior in respect to the former whose love was somehow more carnal?

But that carnal love is worthwhile, since through it sensual love is excluded and the world is condemned and conquered. It becomes better when it is rational and becomes perfect when it is spiritual. Actually it is rational when the reason is so strong in faith that in all things concerning Christ it strays not even in the slightest degree because of any false likeness of truth. Not by any heretical or diabolical deceit does it wander from the integrity of the sense of the Church. In the same way, when speaking on its own it exercises such caution as never to exceed the proper limits of discretion by superstition or frivolity or the vehemence of too eager a spirit. This is loving God with one's whole soul as we said before. If with the help of the Spirit the soul attains such strength that it remains steadfast no matter what the effort or difficulty, if the fear of death itself cannot make it act unjustly but even then it loves with its whole strength, this then is spiritual love. I think the name is very fitting for this special love because of the special fullness of the Spirit in which it excels.

(*Sermons on the Song of Songs* 20:7ff)

Mary, His Mother, Our Advocate

There is no doubt that whatever we say in praise of the mother touches the son and when we honor the son we detract nothing from the mother's glory. For if, as Solomon says, "A wise son is the glory of his father," how much more glorious is it to become the mother of Wisdom himself? But how can I attempt to praise her whom the prophets have proclaimed, the angel has acknowledged, and the evangelist has described as praiseworthy?

(In Praise of the Virgin Mother 4:1)

We may truly call Mary a garden of delights, which the divine South Wind not merely comes and blows upon, but comes down into and blows through, causing the fragrance of its spices, that is, the precious gifts of heavenly grace to flow out and be spread around on every side. Take away from the sky the sun which enlightens the world and what becomes of the day? Take away Mary, this star of life's vast and spacious sea, and what is left to us but a cloud of swirling gloom and a thick and dense darkness? Therefore, my brothers and sisters, with every fiber of our being, every feeling of our hearts, with all the affections of our minds and with all the ardor of our souls, let us honor Mary, because such is the will of God who would have us obtain everything through her hands. Such I say is the will of God who intends it for our benefit.

(Sermon for the Nativity of the Blessed Virgin 6-7)

You have already realized, I suppose, that the Virgin herself is the royal road by which the Savior came to us. Therefore, dear brothers and sisters, let us endeavor to ascend by it to Jesus, who by the same way has come down to us. Let us strive, I say, to go by Mary to share his grace who by Mary came to share our misery. Through you, O most Blessed One, finder of grace, mother of life, mother of salvation, through you let us have access to your Son, so that through you he may receive us, he who was given to us through you.

(Second Sermon for Advent)

Now what is the fountain of life if not Christ the Lord? This stream from the heavenly source descends to us through an aqueduct. The aqueduct does not show all the fullness of the fountain, but it moistens our dry and withered hearts with some few drops of grace, giving more to one, less to another. The aqueduct is always full, so that all may receive of its fullness.

You must have already guessed, dear brothers and sisters, to whom I allude under the image of an aqueduct which, receiving the fullness of the fountain from the Father's heart, has passed it on to us, at least insofar as we can contain it. You know it was she to whom it was said, "Hail, full of grace."

But how did this aqueduct of ours attain to the loftiness of the fountain? How indeed, except by the ardor of her desires, by the fervor of her devotion, by the purity of her prayer? How did she reach up even to the inaccessible Majesty but by knocking, by asking, by seeking? And she found what she was seeking, since it was said to her: "You have found favor with God."

(Sermon for the Nativity of the Blessed Virgin Mary 6)

Let us now say a few words about this name, which means "star of the sea" and is so becoming the Virgin Mother. Surely she is very fittingly likened to a star. . . . O you, whoever you are, who feel that in the tidal wave of this world you are nearer to being tossed about among the squalls and gales than treading on dry land, if you do not want to founder in the tempest, do not avert your eyes from the brightness of the star. When the wind of temptation blows up within you, when you strike upon the rock of tribulation, gaze up at the star, call out to Mary. Whether you are being tossed about by the waves of pride or ambition or slander or jealousy, gaze up at this star, call out to Mary. When rage or greed or fleshly desires are battering the skiff of your soul, gaze up at Mary. When the immensity of your sins weighs you down and you are bewildered by the loathesomeness of your conscience, when the terrifying thought of judgment appalls you and you begin to founder in the gulf of sadness and despair, think of Mary. In dangers, in hardships, in every doubt, think of Mary, call out to Mary. Keep her in your mouth, keep her in your heart. Follow the example of her life and you obtain the favor of her prayer. Following her, you will never go astray. Asking her help, you will never despair. Keeping her in your thoughts, you will never wander away. With your hand in hers, you will never stumble. With her protecting you, you will not be afraid. With her leading you, you will never tire.

Her kindness will see you through to the end. Then you will know from your own experience how true it is that "the Virgin's name was Mary."

(In Praise of the Virgin Mary 2:17)

Ladders

The spiritual fathers and mothers, the saints of old, and the spiritual writers of today have used many images to depict the spiritual journey. Perhaps best known in our time are the interior castle of Teresa of Jesus, with its many mansions, and John of the Cross' Mount Carmel with its various ascents. A favorite of the Cistercian Fathers was the eight beatitudes found in the Gospel of Matthew at the beginning of the Sermon on the Mount. Bernard of Clairvaux used the eight beatitudes along with many others images: the three steps of truth and the four degrees of love, as we shall see here; the seven infusions of the Holy Spirit; the three ages of the spiritual life; the four stages of organic growth, etc. But a favorite by far from the earliest times, inspired by the scriptures, has been the image of the ladder.

However, it was perhaps duty more than choice that brought Bernard to the twelve steps in this very early treatise. As a Cistercian abbot he was expected each morning to speak to his monks, commenting on Benedict's *Rule for Monasteries*. This brought him quickly enough to the twelve-rung ladder used by Benedict to describe the way of humility in the seventh chapter of his *Rule*. Bernard's verbal commentary, found here only in briefest form, must have brought great smiles to his monks' faces as well as much insight to their lives. When he sent off his prior, Godfrey of Langres, as head of Clairvaux's second foundation, Fontenay, the one request Godfrey made of his friend and abbot was a transcript of these talks. Friendship has its

43

demands. Bernard wrote the treatise in his own inimitable way, humbly choosing the negative image of the steps of pride. For this reason it perhaps speaks more immediately to all of us.

As Bernard makes clear, the first step on the spiritual journey is in fact wherever we are. We can locate ourselves on the ladder of pride and begin from there. No matter how far down on the ladder of pride we are, we can, on that very rung, turn around and begin the ascent toward the fullness of humility, which is none other than the truth about ourselves.

Once we get to this platform we are already on the first step of truth. As Bernard makes clear, this is precisely why we need the ladder of humility and climb it: to get to the truth. The truth about ourselves inevitably leads to compassion for others: We are all a bunch of struggling sinners, each on his or her own step of pride, each called to the ascent. Compassion expresses itself in mercy. And the merciful see God. That's the way it works. We do not so much need to understand it as to live it. Seeing God, we are ready for contemplation, the enjoyment of God, the refreshing rest of communion.

There is a growth in this seeing of God. This Bernard draws out for us in the steps of love. But first we get in touch with the rich humanism of this spiritual father. The first step of love is love of ourselves. There is a good self love and it is foundational. It corresponds to the first degree of truth: knowing ourselves, poor, weak, stupid sinners but still the very image of God, the beloved of God's creating. We begin to realize God's goodness to us and love him for that. Then we begin to perceive how good he is in himelf and love him just because he is so good. Love brings about union. We begin to see things his way, to love things as he loves them, to love even ourselves because he loves us. We have come to be one with God in mind and heart. And all the fullness of the divine joy is ours.

These are Bernard's ladders with their steps. They can guide us, give us some help in discerning our way, encourage us on the ascent.

A Ladder That Goes Up and Down

Before I speak of the different steps of humility — which indeed Saint Benedict does not ask us to count but to climb — I will first try to show what we may expect to find at the top. The toil will be easier if we have the profit before our eyes.

Our Lord shows us plainly both the difficulty and the reward of the work. "I am the Way, the Truth and the Life." The way is humility, the goal is truth. The first is the labor, the second the reward. But you may ask: "How do I know that he is speaking of humility when he only uses a general word, 'I am the Way'?" Well, I will give you a clearer text: "Learn of me for I am meek and humble of heart." He points to himself as an example of humility, a model of meekness. Imitate him and you will not walk in darkness but will have the light of life. What is the light of life but truth that enlightens every person who comes into this world and shows us where the true life is to be found? So, when he says: "I am the Way and the Truth," he adds, "and the Life." It is as if he said: "I am the Way, I lead to Truth; I am the Truth, I promise Life; and I myself am the very Life I give you." "For this is eternal life, that they may know you the one true God and Jesus Christ whom you have sent."

Supposing, then, that you go on to object: "I see the way — humility; I long for the goal to which it leads — Truth, but what if the way is so difficult that I can never reach the goal?" The answer comes promptly: "I am the Life," that is, I am food, the viaticum, to sustain you on your journey.

There are some who go astray and cannot find the road. He cries to them: "I am the Way." Some doubt and waver in their faith. His word to them is: "I am the Truth." To those who grow weary with the climbing, his cry is this: "I am the Life."

To define humility: Humility is a virtue by which one has a low opinion of one's self because one knows one's self well. This is the virtue that belongs to those who have set their hearts to climb and have gone from virtue to virtue, from step to step, until they have reached the highest peak of humility and have gazed upon Truth from the watchtower of Zion. "For the Lawgiver will give a blessing." This means that he who gives the law is the same who gives the blessing; he who commands humility will lead safely to the Truth. Who is this Lawgiver? Who but the good and sweet Lord who gives a law to those who wander from the way? They wander from the way because they have gone astray from the truth. Will they then be deserted by our sweet Lord? No, the law that this good kind Lord gives them is the way of humility by which they can return to the knowledge of the truth.

This law which points to the way back to truth Saint Benedict sums up in twelve steps. Just as the ten commandments of the Law and the twofold circumcision — which add up to twelve — lead to Christ, so do these twelve steps, which we have to climb to come to the possession of Truth. This was the ladder which was shown to Jacob — a figure of humility. Leaning on the top of the ladder the Lord looks on the children of the human family with eyes of truth, that deceive not and cannot be deceived, to see if there is any who understands and seeks God. His place at the ladder's top shows us that the knowledge of truth is to be found at the summit of humility.

Yes, the way of humility is a good way. It seeks for truth, it wins charity, it shares the fruits of wisdom. Just as the end of the Law is Christ, so the perfection of humility is the knowledge of truth. When Christ came he brought grace; when truth is known it brings love. To the humble it is known. "He gives his grace to the humble."

(*The Steps of Humility and Pride* 1ff)

Of all his virtues, and he possessed them all, Christ specially commends one to us, humility. "Learn of me for I am meek and humble of heart."

How glad I, too, should be, Lord Jesus, to glory, if I could, in my infirmity that your virtue, your humility might be made perfect in me. Your grace is sufficient for me when my own virtue fails. With the foot of grace firmly planted on the ladder of humility, painfully dragging the foot of my own weakness behind me, I should safely mount upward, until, holding fast to the truth, I attained the broad plain of charity. There I shall sing my song of thanksgiving: "You have set my feet on a broad plain." Thus I warily enter on the narrow way, step by step safely ascend the steep ladder, and by a kind of miracle climb to the truth, behind the time perhaps, and limping, but still with confidence. "Woe is me that my exile is prolonged. Oh, that I had wings like a dove, that I might fly away" to truth and be at rest in charity! But since I have no wings, "lead me in your way, O Lord, that I may walk in your truth" and the truth will make me free. Why did I ever desert the truth? If I had not been so light-headed and stupid as to come down from truth I would not now be faced with this slow and hard climb back to it. Did I say, "come down"? "Crash down" would be more like it. Though in a certain sense the milder expression is more suitable because one does not plunge to the depths of evil in one sudden fall, no more than one springs to the heights of virtue at one bound but has to climb step by step. So the descent, too, is spread out little by little, according to the picture given to us: "The wicked are proud all the days of their life." And, "There are ways that seem to us right, but their end leads to evil."

You see now there is a way down and a way up, a way to evil and a way to good. Yes, and it is in that hope that I have chosen the path of truth, to climb by it, now that I am humbled, to the place from which I fell in my pride. Yes, I will climb back and I will sing: "It is good for me, Lord, that you have humbled me.

The same ladder is for those who come down the way of iniquity, for those who go up the way of truth. By the same steps one goes up to the throne and one comes down from it, by the same road one goes to the city and one departs from it; by the same gate one enters and one leaves the house. Indeed, it was by the one same ladder that Jacob saw the angels ascending and descending.

What is the bearing of all this? It is that when you wish to return to the truth there is no need to seek an unknown road. It is the same as that by which you came down. On your ascent you will be able to follow the track of the footprints you made in your descent. Now that you are humbled you will climb by the same steps you trod on as you came down in your pride. The twelfth and lowest step to which your pride brought you is the first step upwards of humility and so on in due order: the eleventh is the second, the tenth the third, the ninth the fourth, the eighth the fifth, the seventh the sixth, the sixth the seventh, the fifth the eighth, the fourth the ninth, the third the tenth, the second the eleventh, the first the twelfth. If your conscience has noted these steps of your pride, you will recognize them and will have no trouble in finding the way of humility.

(*The Steps of Humility and Pride* 25ff)

The first step of pride: curiosity

The first step of pride is curiosity. How does it show itself? Now you begin to notice that wherever you are, standing, walking or sitting, your eyes are wondering, your glance darts right and left, your ears are cocked. Some change has taken place in you, every movement shows it. "The perverse person winks the eye, nudges the foot, points the finger." These symptoms show your soul has caught some disease. You used to watch over your own conduct, now all your watchfulness is for others. "They do not know themselves so they must go forth to pasture their goats." Goats are a symbol of sin, and I am applying the word to their eyes and ears. They are the windows through which death creeps into the soul, as death came into the world by sin. These are the flocks the curious tend while they let their soul starve.

My friend, if you gave yourself the attention you ought, I do not think you would have much time to look after others. Listen, busybody, to Solomon. Listen to the words of the Wise Man for a fool: "Guard your heart with all care." Your senses have quite enough to do to guard the source of life. You wander away from yourself? Whom have you left in charge? Your eyes sweep the heavens. How do you dare, you who have sinned against heaven? Look over the earth, that you might know yourself. It speaks to you of yourself, because "dust you are and unto dust you shall return."

Are the eyes never to be raised at all?

Yes, but only for two reasons: to look for help or to help others. David raised his eyes to the mountains to see if help would come to him. Our Lord looked out over the crowd to see if they needed his help. One raised his eyes in misery, the other in mercy — two excellent reasons. If when time, place and circumstances call for it, you raise your eyes for your own need or your sister's or brother's, I certainly will not blame you. I will think all the better of you. Misery is a good excuse. Mercy is a very commendable reason.

If it is for some motive other than these two that you raise your eyes I am afraid you imitate neither the prophet [David] nor our Lord but Dinah, Eve or Satan himself.

Dinah was leading her goats to pasture when she was snatched away from her father and despoiled of her virginity.

Ah! Dinah! You were anxious to see the foreign women? What need was there for that? What good did it do you? Was it just idle curiosity? Yes, you were idle, but someone who saw you did not stay idle. You were looking about curiously, but someone eyed you still more curiously. Who would have then believed that your curious idleness or idle curiosity would be fruitful. But it did bear terrible fruit for you and for your family and for your enemies, too.

What about you, Eve? You were in paradise, charged along with your husband to tend it and care for it. If you had kept the command given you, you would have gone in due time to a better place where there is no labor and no care. You were permitted to eat the fruit of every tree except the tree of knowledge of good and evil. The other trees were good, and their fruit tasted well. Why did you want the fruit that tasted evil as well? "Be not wiser than it behaves one to be wise." To be wise in evil is not wisdom but foolishness. Keep what is entrusted to you, wait for what is promised to you. Avoid what is forbidden or you will lose what you already have. Why are you so ready to look on death? What do those glances mean? You are forbidden to eat that fruit, why do you look at it?

"Oh!" you answer. "I am only looking. I have not so much as put a hand to it. My eyes are under no restriction. I was forbidden only to eat. What did God give me eyes for if I cannot look at whatever I want?"

Have you never read: "All things are lawful for me but not all expedient?" The look may not have been a sin itself but there was a sin somewhere in the background. You cannot have been watching very carefully over yourself or you would not have had time for this curiosity. It may not itself be a sin but it is leading you on to sin. You are already guilty of some fault in the matter and more will follow. While your attention was taken up with this the serpent quietly slipped into your heart, and his soft words are being spoken, gentle persuasive words, lies to lull fears to sleep. "No, you will not die," he says. He strengthens your attention, he rouses your appetite, he whets your curiosity, he stirs up your greed. While he presents you with a forbidden fruit he steals the gift you have been given. He gave you an apple and stole paradise. You drink the poison. You will die and be the mother of the dying. Before the first child was born salvation was gone. We are born and we die. We are born dying men and women, for the doom of death is laid upon us before ever we are born. This is the heavy burden you have laid upon all your sons and daughters even to this day.

And you, Satan! Made in the likeness of God, placed not in Eden but in the delights of the Paradise of God, what more did you want? Full of wisdom and perfect beauty, seek not what is too high for you, peer not into what is too mighty. Stay in your own place lest you fall if you walk in great and wonderful things above you. Why are you casting those glances toward the North? I see you musing very earnestly on something. I do not know what it is but it is something beyond your reach. You say: "I will place my throne in the North." All others in heaven's courts are standing, you alone presume to sit. You disturb the concord of your fellows, the peace of the heavenly country, and if it were possible even the peace of the Blessed Trinity. Wretch! To this your curiosity has led you. With reckless insolence you shock your fellow-citizens and insult your King. "Thousands of thousands minister to him, ten times a hundred

thousand stand before him." In that court none has a right
to sit save him who sits above the Cherubim, waited on by
all. In an unheard-of way you would distinguish yourself
from others. You pry with insatiable curiosity, push yourself
forward without respect and place your throne in heaven
and make yourself the equal of the Most High.

(The Steps of Humility and Pride 28ff)

The sum total is: Satan fell from truth by curiosity when
he turned his attention to something he coveted unlawfully
and had the presumption to believe he could gain it.
Curiosity was the beginning of all sin and so is rightly
considered the first step of pride. Unless it is checked
promptly it leads to the second step: levity.

The second step of pride: levity of mind

You who observe others instead of attending to your self
will begin before long to see some as your superiors and
others as your inferiors. In some you will see things to envy;
in others, things to despise. The eyes have wandered and
the mind soon follows. It is no longer steadily fixed on its
real concerns and is now carried up on the crest of the waves
of pride, now down in the trough of envy. One minute you
are full of envious sadness, the next childishly glad about
some excellence you see in yourself. The former is evil; the
latter, vain. Both bespeak pride, because it is love of one's
own excellence that makes you weep when you are sur-
passed and rejoice in surpassing others. Your conversation
will show how your mind is tossed up and down. One
moment you are sulky and silent except for some bitter
remarks, the next sees a full spate of silly chatter. Now you
are laughing, now doleful, all without rhyme or reason.

We will proceed to the third step of pride — to teach it, not, I hope, to practice it.

The third step of pride: giddiness

The proud always seek what is pleasant and try to avoid what is troublesome. In the words of scripture: "Where there is gladness, there is the heart of a fool." Having come down the two steps of curiosity and levity of mind, you will find much to upset you. You are saddened every time you see the goodness of others. Impatient with humiliation, you find an escape in false consolations. Your eyes are closed to anything that shows your own vileness or the excellence of others, wide open to what flatters yourself. You are largely saved now from your moody exaltation and depression, you have retired into a happy cloud-land. This is the third step. There are indications by which you can know when you yourself or another have reached this point. Watch yourself and you will never notice anything like a tear or a sigh. Your appearance is that of a person who is forgetful of what you are or at least one now purified of all trace of sin. You are scurrilous, over cheerful in appearance, swaggering in bearing, always ready for a joke, any little thing quickly gets a laugh. You are careful not to remember anything you have done which could hurt your self-esteem. But all your good points will be remembered and added up and, if need be, touched up by imagination. You think only of what you want and never of what is permitted. At times you simply cannot stop laughing or hide your empty-headed merriment. You are like a well-filled bladder that has been pricked and squeezed. The air, not finding a free vent, whistles out through the little hole with squeak after squeak. Vain thoughts and silly jokes gather pressure inside until they burst out in giggles. In embarrassment you bury your face in your hands, tighten your lips, clench your teeth. It is no use! The laughter must burst out and if your hand holds it in your mouth, it bursts out through your nose.

The fourth step of pride: boasting

When vanity has swelled the bladder to its limits, a bigger vent must be made or the bladder will burst. As your silly merriment grows, laughing is not enough outlet. You say like Elihu: "Behold, my heart is like new wine that has no vent, like new wineskins it is ready to burst." Yes, speak or burst! You are full of words and the swelling spirit strains within you. Your hunger and thirst are for listeners, someone to listen to your boasting, on whom you can pour out all your thoughts, someone you can show what a big person you are.

At last the chance to speak comes. The discussion turns on literature. You bring forth from your treasury old things and new. You are not shy about producing your opinions, words are bubbling over. You do not wait to be asked. Your information comes before any question. You ask the questions, give the answers, cut off anyone who tries to speak. When the time comes and it is necessary to interrupt the conversation, hour-long though it be, you seek a minute more. You must get leave to resume your talk, not to edify your listeners, but to show off your learning. You may have the capacity to help others, but that is the least of your concerns. Your aim is not to teach nor to be taught, but to show how much you know. If the conversation brings up the subject of religion, you are quite ready to talk of visions and dreams. You warmly recommend fasting, urge watching and exalt prayer above all. You will give a long discourse on patience and humility and each of the other virtues — all words, all bragging. You trust that they will draw the conclusion "out of the abundance of the heart the mouth speaks" or "a good person from a good treasure brings forth good things." The talk takes a lighter turn. You are more in your element here and become really eloquent. As they hear you, they will say your mouth has become a fountain of wit, a river of smart talk. You can get the most grave and serious laughing heartily. To say it briefly, when words are many, boasting is not lacking. There is the fourth step described and identified. Flee the reality but remember the name. The same warning goes with the next, which I name singularity.

The fifth step of pride: singularity

When you have been bragging that you are better than others you would feel ashamed of yourself if you did not live up to your boast and show how much better than others you are. You do not so much want to be better as to be seen to be better. You are not so much concerned about leading a better life as appearing to others to do so. You can then say: "I am not like the rest of men." You are more complacent about fasting for one day when the others are feasting than about fasting seven days with all the rest. While you are at your meals you cast your eyes around the tables and if you see anyone eating less than yourself you are mortified at being outdone and promptly and cruelly deprive yourself of even necessary food. You would rather starve your body than your pride. If you see anyone more thin, anyone more pallid, you despise yourself. You are never at rest. You wonder what others think about the appearance of your face, whether it is rosy or wan, poking at your ribs and feeling your shoulders and loins to see how skinny or fleshy they are.

Some of the more simple-minded are misled by your worthless singularities and, judging by your actions which

they see and not seeing the hidden intentions, they canon-
ize the unfortunate one and confirm you in your self-delu-
sion.

The sixth step of pride: self-conceit

You swallow all the praise others give you. You are quite
complacent about your conduct and you never examine
your motives now. The good opinion of others is all you
need. About everything else you think you know more than
anybody, but when they say something favorable about
you, you believe them against your own conscience. So now
not only in words and affected conduct do you display your
piety but you believe in your inmost heart that you are
holier than others. It never occurs to you that the praise
given to you comes from ignorance or kindness. Your pride
thinks it only your due. So, after singularity, self-conceit
comes sixth, and the seventh is presumption.

The seventh step of pride: presumption

When you think you are better than others will you not
put yourself before others? You must have the first place in
gatherings, be the first to speak. You come without being
called. You interfere without being asked. You must arrange
everything, re-do whatever has been done. What you yourself did not do or arrange is not rightly done or properly
arranged. You are the judge of all judges and decide every
case beforehand. If you are called to some ordinary task you
refuse disdainfully. A person fitted for higher positions
could not be occupied with lesser things.

Since you are so liberal, even reckless, in offering your
services, sooner or later you will make some blunders. Will

you admit your fault? You could hardly believe that you could be wrong and certainly will not let anybody else believe it. Thus your fault is made worse instead of being set right. If therefore, when you are corrected, you see yourself making excuses in your sin, you will know that you have dropped another step — the eighth, which is named self-justification.

The eighth step of pride: self-justification

There are many ways of excusing sins. One will say: "I didn't do it." Another: "I did it, but I was perfectly right in doing it." If it was wrong you may say: "It isn't all that bad." If it was decidedly harmful, you can fall back on: "I meant well." If the bad intention is too evident you will take refuge in the excuses of Adam and Eve and say someone else led you into it. If you defend your obvious sins like that, you are hardly likely to make known in humble confession the evil thoughts of your heart and the sins you have committed in secret.

The ninth step of pride: hypocritical confession

Excuses of this kind are bad enough for the psalmist to call them "words of malice," but there is something even more dangerous than this stubborn and obstinate self-defence, and that is hypocritical confession springing from pride. There are some who, when they are caught out in wrong-doing and know that if they defend themselves they will not be believed, find a subtle way out of the difficulty in deceitful self-accusation. These are the kind of persons "who humble themselves deceitfully while their minds are full of evil." Their eyes are cast down, they humble themselves to the very dust. They wring out some tears if they can, sighs and groans interrupt their words. They will not merely admit what has happened but will exaggerate their guilt. They accuse themselves of things so great, so incredible, that you begin to doubt the charges you were certain of before. The things they say about themselves now can surely not be true, perhaps the other things are not so certain either. They are making statements they do not want you to believe, they defend the fault by confessing and hide it by false openness. The confession sounds very well but evil is hidden in the heart. The hearer is led to think that the accusation is not really true, it is only humility. After all, the scripture says: "The just person is the first to accuse self." Such persons are willing that you think they are telling lies about themselves so long as you do not think they are failing in humility. They will not get much credit from God for either truth or humility. If their guilt is too great for any defence, they will assume the attitude of penitents hoping that their fault will be forgotten in admiration of their candid confession. But the candor of their confession is all in outward show. It does not come from the heart and cancels no sin.

Pride is certainly paying a compliment to humility if it uses it as a disguise when it would escape punishment.

An earthen vessel is tested by fire and the true penitent by tribulation. Real penitents are not afraid of the difficulties of penance. Whatever is enjoined upon them for their fault which they hate, they patiently embrace with a quiet mind. Those whose penitence is fraudulent will show soon enough that it was a sham humility if they are given the slightest reproach or penance. They murmur and growl and get vexed. No, they are not in the fourth degree of humility but the ninth of pride, which we have called hypocritical confession. You can judge for yourself what is the state of these proud persons' minds. Their fraud has failed them, their peace of mind is gone, their reputation has been lowered, and their sin is unforgiven. Now everybody knows what they are. Not only does everyone condemn them, but all are more vexed because of the good opinion they held so long because they were fooled by the fraud.

The tenth step of pride: revolt

The divine mercy may yet rescue such and inspire them to submit to the judgment of the community, but such a character finds this a very hard thing to do. Instead they may take an attitude of brazen insolence and in exasperation take the fatal plunge as far as the tenth step of pride. They have already shown contempt for their brothers and sisters by insolence, and now their contempt for the authority of the Church flashes out in open revolt.

The eleventh step of pride: freedom to sin

Those in revolt have reached the tenth step of pride and will leave. Without delay they go down to the eleventh step. They then set their feet on ways that seem to them right but which will lead them, if God does not block their way, to the depths of hell, to contempt of God. "When the wicked reach the depths of evil, they are full of contempt." We may style this eleventh step freedom in sinning. With fewer qualms they happily give themselves up to their sinful desires. They still keep some scant fear of God. Their consciences still give some murmurs, however faint. They make a few half-hearted resolutions, still hesitate a little in their first steps in evil. They do not plunge headlong into the torrent of vice but feel their way step by step like one trying a ford.

The twelfth step of pride: the habit of sinning

The first steps in sin are taken apprehensively and no blow falls from the dreaded judgment of God. Pleasure in sin has been experienced. Sin is repeated and the pleasure grows. Old desires revive, conscience is dulled, habit tightens its grip. The unfortunate ones sink into the evil depths, are tangled in their vices and are swept into the whirlpool of sinful longings while their reason and the fear of God are forgotten. "The fool says in his heart: There is no God." God or evil means nothing to them now. They are ready to serve sin heart, hand and foot with thoughts, acts and plans unchecked. They seek new ways of sinning. The plans of the heart, the ready words of the mouth, the works of the hand are at the service of every impulse. They have become malevolent, evil-speaking, vile.

The just who have climbed all the steps of humility run on to life with a ready heart and with the ease of good habit. The evil who have dropped down to the bottom are ruled by evil habit and unchecked by fear they run boldly on to death. Those in mid-course, whether going up or down, are weary with the strain, torn now by the fear of hell and now by the attraction of old habits. Only at the top and at the bottom is there a free and effortless course, upward to life and downward to death, bounding on in the effortless energy of love or hurried, unresisting by the downward pull of stupidity. In one case love, in the other apathy ignores the labor of life. Perfect love or complete malice cast out fear. Security is found in truth or in blindness. So we can call the twelfth step the habit of sinning by which the fear of God has been lost, replaced by contempt.

(*The Steps of Humility and Pride* 38ff)

It looks as if I have described the steps of pride rather than those of humility. All I can say is that I can teach only what I know myself. I could not very well describe the way up because I am more used to falling down than to climbing. Saint Benedict describes the steps of humility to you because he had them in his heart. I can only tell you what I know myself, the downward path. However, if you study this carefully you will find the way up. If you are going to Rome who can tell you the way better than one you meet coming from there? Such a one will describe the towns, villages, cities, rivers and mountains passed, and as you go along you will meet and recognize them in the reverse order. So, in our downward journey you will discover the steps that will lead you up. As you climb them you will see them better from your own experience than from the description of our book.

(The Steps of Humility and Pride 57)

The Steps of Truth

There are three degrees in the perception of truth. We must look for truth in ourselves, in our neighbor, in itself. We look for truth in ourselves when we judge ourselves, in our neighbor when we have sympathy for their sufferings, in itself when we contemplate it with a clean heart.

It is important to observe the order of these degrees as well as their number. First of all, truth teaches us that we must look for it in our neighbors before we seek it in itself. You will then see easily why you must seek it in yourself before you seek it in your neighbors. In the list of the beatitudes the merciful are spoken of before the clean of heart. The merciful quickly grasp the truth in their neighbors when their heart goes out to them with a love that unites them so closely that they feel their neighbors' good and ill as if it were their own. With the weak they are weak, with the scandalized they are on fire. They rejoice with those who rejoice and weep with those who weep. Their hearts are made more clear-sighted by love, and they experience the delight of contemplating truth, not now in others but in itself, and for love of it they bear their neighbors' sorrow. Those who do not live in harmony with their brothers and sisters, who mock at those who weep and sneer at those who are glad, have no sympathy with them because their feelings do not affect them. They can never really see the truth in others. The proverb fits them well: The sound person feels not the sick one's pains, nor the well-fed the pangs of the hungry. It is fellow sufferers that readily feel compassion for the sick and the hungry. For just as pure truth is seen only by the pure of heart, so also a brother's or sister's miseries are truly experienced only by one who has misery in one's own heart. You will never have real mercy for the failings of another until you know and realize that you have the same failings in your soul. Our Savior has given us the example. He willed to suffer so that he might know compassion. To learn mercy he shared our misery. It is written: "He learned obedience from the things he suffered." And he learned mercy in the same way. I do not mean that he did not know how to be merciful before. His mercy is from eternity to eternity. But what in his divine nature he knows from all eternity he learned by experience in time.

(The Steps of Humility and Pride 6)

If Jesus submitted himself to human misery so that he might not simply know of it but experience it as well, how much more ought you not make any change in your condition but pay attention to what you are, because you are truly full of misery. This is the only way, if you are to learn to be merciful. If you have eyes for the shortcomings of your neighbor and not for your own, no feeling of mercy will arise in you but rather indignation. You will be more ready to judge than to help, to crush in the spirit of anger than to instruct in the spirit of gentleness. "You who are spirited, instruct such a one in the spirit of gentleness," says the apostle [Paul]. His counsel, or better, his precept is that you should treat an ailing brother or sister with the spirit of gentleness with which you would like to be treated yourself in your weakness. He shows then how to find out the right way to apply this spirit of gentleness: "Considering yourself lest you also be tempted."

It is worth noticing that the Disciple of Truth follows the order of his master's thoughts. As I have said, just as in the beatitudes the merciful come before the clean of heart, so the meek are spoken of before the merciful. When the apostle tells the spiritually minded to instruct the earthly minded he adds: "In the spirit of meekness." The only ones who can instruct brothers and sisters are those who are merciful, those who are meek and humble. In other words, one cannot really be merciful if one is not humble. Thus the apostle clearly shows what I promised to prove to you, namely that we must look for truth first in ourselves and afterward in our neighbor. "Considering yourself," he says, that is, considering how easily you are tempted and how prone to sin, you will become meek and ready to help others in the "spirit of gentleness."

If the words of the disciple do not impress you enough, perhaps you will take warning from the stern words of the master: "Hypocrite, first cast the beam from your own eye and then you will see better to cast the mote from your brother's or sister's." The heavy, thick beam in the eye is pride of heart. It is big but not strong, swollen but not solid. It blinds the eye of the mind and blots out the truth. While it is there, you cannot see yourself as you really are or even see the ideal of what you would be, but you think you are or hope to be what you would like to be.

(*The Steps of Humility and Pride* 13f)

If you want to know the full truth about yourself, you will have to get rid of the beam of pride which blocks out the light from your eye, and then set up in your heart a ladder of humility so that you can search into yourself.

When you have climbed its twelve steps you will then stand on the first step of truth. When you have seen the truth about yourself, or better, when you have seen yourself in the truth, you will be able to say: "I believed, therefore I have spoken, but I have been exceedingly humbled." It is as if you said with the psalmist: Because I have not been ashamed to confess the known truth about myself, I have attained to the perfection of humility. We can think of this as saying: When as yet I did not fully know the truth, I thought myself something, whereas I was nothing. But when I came to know Christ, to imitate his humility I saw the truth and exalted it in me by my confession, but "I myself was humbled exceedingly." In my own eyes, I fell very low. The psalmist has been humbled and now stands on the first step of truth.

When in the light of truth people know themselves and so think less of themselves, it will certainly follow that what they loved before will now become bitter to them. They are brought face to face with themselves and blush at what they see. Their present state is no pleasure to them. They aspire to something better and at the same time realize how little they can rely on themselves to achieve it. It hurts them and they find some relief in judging themselves severely. Love of truth makes them hunger and thirst after justice and conceive a deep contempt for themselves. They are anxious to exact from themselves full satisfaction and real amendment. They admit that to make satisfaction is beyond their own powers — when they have done all that is commanded them they acknowledge that they are still unprofitable servants. They fly from justice to mercy, by the road Truth shows them: "Blessed are the merciful for they shall obtain mercy." They look beyond their own needs to the needs of their neighbors, and from the things they themselves have suffered they learn compassion: They have come to the second degree of truth.

If they persevere in these things—sorrow of repentance, desire for justice, and works of mercy—they will cleanse their hearts from the three impediments of ignorance, weakness and jealousy and will come through contemplation to the third degree of truth.

(The Steps of Humility and Pride 15ff)

These are the three steps of truth. We climb to the first by the toil of humility, to the second by the deep feelings of compassion, and to the third by the ecstasy of contemplation. On the first step we experience the severity of truth, on the second its tenderness, on the third its purity. Reason brings us to the first as we judge ourselves; compassion brings us to the second when we have mercy on others; on the third the purity of truth sweeps us up to the sight of things invisible.

It occurs to me here that it is possible to allot each of these three works to one of the Persons of the undivided Trinity, that is, insofar as we, still sitting in darkness, can make any distinctions in the world of the three Persons who always work as One. There would seem to be something characteristic of the Son in the first stage, of the Holy Spirit in the second, of the Father in the third. What is the work of the Son? "If I, your Lord and Master have washed your feet, how much more ought you also to wash each other's feet." The Master of truth gave his disciples an example of humility and opened to them the first stage of truth. Then the work of the Holy Spirit: "Charity is spread abroad in our hearts by the Holy Spirit who is given to us." Charity is a gift of the Holy Spirit. Those who under the instruction of the Son were led to the first step of truth through humility, now under the guidance of the Holy Spirit reach the second stage through compassion for their neighbor.

Finally, listen to what is said of the Father: "Blessed are you, Simon, son of Jonah, for flesh and blood have not revealed this to you but my Father who is in heaven." Again: "The Father will make known the truth to the sons." And "I confess to you, Father, for you have hidden these things from the wise and made them known to little ones." You see, by word and example the Son first teaches humility, then the Spirit pours out his charity upon those whom the Father receives finally into glory. The Son makes them his disciples, the Spirit consoles them as friends, the Father bestows on them the glory of sons and daughters. However, truth is the proper title, not of the Son alone but of the Spirit and the Father too, so that it must be made quite clear, while giving full acknowledgement to the properties of Persons, that it is the one truth who works at all these stages: in the first teaching as a Master, in the second consoling as a Friend and Brother, in the third embracing as a Father.

The Son of God, the Word and Wisdom of the Father, mercifully assumed to himself human reason, the first of our powers. He found it oppressed by the flesh, held captive by sin, blinded by ignorance, distracted by outward things. He raised it by his might, taught it by his wisdom, drew it to things interior. More wonderfully still, he delegated to it his own power of judge. To judge is the proper act of truth, and in this it shared when out of reverence for the Word to which it is joined it became accuser, witness and judge against itself. Humility had been born from the union of the Word with human reason. Then the Holy Spirit lovingly visited the second power, the will. He found it rotten with the infection of the flesh but already judged by reason. Gently he cleansed it, made it burn with affection, made it merciful until, like a skin made pliable with oil, it would spread abroad the heavenly oil of love even to its enemies. The union of the Holy Spirit with the human will gives birth to charity. See now this perfect soul, its two powers, the reason and the will, without spot or wrinkle, the reason instructed by the Word of truth, the will inflamed by truth's Spirit. Sprinkled with the hyssop of humility, fired with the flame of charity, cleansed from spot by humility, smoothed of wrinkles by charity, the reason never shrinking from the truth, the will never striving against reason, this blessed soul the Father binds to himself as his own glorious bride.

Now the reason is no longer preoccupied with itself and the will is no longer concerned with others, for the blessed soul is lost in one delight: "The King has led me into his chamber." The soul has become worthy of this when she learned humility in the school of the Son, listening to the warning: "If you do not know yourself, go forth and pasture your flocks." She is twice worthy since she was led by the Holy Spirit from the school of humility to the storehouse of charity, for this is what is meant by guarding the flocks of the neighbors. She was brought there by love. Once there, she is cushioned by flowers, stayed up with apples, that is, by good morals and holy virtues. And finally she is led into the chamber of the King for whose love she languishes. There for a short time, just one half-hour, while there is silence in heaven, she sleeps in the desired embrace. She sleeps but her heart watches and is fed with the secrets of truth on which later, when she comes to herself, her memory can dwell. There she sees things invisible and hears things unspeakable, which it is not given us to utter. They are beyond the knowledge which night can pass onto night, for this is the word that day utters to day. Wise persons speak wisdom to the wise, and spiritual things are made known to the spiritual.

(*The Steps of Humility and Pride* 19ff)

I have quite work enough for my hands and feet beneath the lowest heaven. Thanks to the help of him who called me I have built a ladder to take me to it. This is my road to God's salvation. Already I see God, resting on the top of the ladder, already I have the joy of hearing the voice of Truth. He calls to me and I reply to him: "Stretch out your right hand to the work of your hands." You have numbered my steps, O Lord, but I am a slow climber, a weary traveler, and I need a resting place. Woe is me if the darkness should overtake me or if my flight should be in winter or on the Sabbath, seeing that now, in an acceptable time, on the day of salvation, I can hardly grope my way to the light. Why am I so slow? Oh, if anyone is to me a son or daughter, a brother or sister in the Lord, a comrade, one who shares my journey, let that one pray for me!

(*The Steps of Humility and Pride* 24)

The Steps of Love

You wish me to tell you why and how much God should be loved. My answer is: The reason for loving God is God; the measure, to love without measure.

There are two reasons why God should be loved for his own sake: No one can be loved more justly and no one can be loved more fruitfully.

When it is asked why God should be loved, there are two meanings possible to the question. It can be asked, for what merit of his or for what advantage of ours is God to be loved. My answer to both questions is the same: I can see no other reason for loving him than himself.

So first let us see for what merit of his he is to be loved. God certainly merits a lot from us since he gave himself to us when we deserved it least. Besides, what could he have given us better than himself? Hence, when seeking why God should be loved, if one asks what right he has to be loved, the answer is that the main reason for loving him is that "he loved us first." Surely he is worthy of being loved in return when one thinks of who loves, whom he loved, and how much he loves. Is it not he whom every spirit acknowledges, saying: "You are my God, you do not need my goods." This divine love is sincere, for it is the love of one who does not seek his own advantage. To whom is such love shown? It is written: "Although we were his enemies up to then, we were reconciled to God." Thus God loved, and freely so, his enemies. How much did he love? John answers: "God so loved the world that he gave his only-begotten Son." And Paul adds: "He did not spare his own Son but delivered him up for us." The Son also said of himself: " No one has greater love than that he lay down his life for his friends."

(*On Loving God* 1)

The first step of love:
We love ourselves for our own sake

Love is one of the four natural passions. There is no need to name them for they are well known. It would be right, however, for that which is natural to be first of all at the author of nature's service. That is why the first and greatest commandment is: "You should love the Lord your God. . . ."

Since nature has become more fragile and weak, necessity obliges us to serve it first. This is carnal love by which we love ourselves above all for our own sake. We are only aware of ourselves. As it is written: "What is animal came first, then what was spiritual." Love is not imposed by a precept, it is implanted in our nature. Who is there that hates his own flesh? Yet should love, as it happens, grow immoderate and, like a savage current, burst the banks of necessity, flooding the fields of delight, the overflow is immediately stopped by the commandment which says: "You shall love your neighbor as yourself." It is just indeed that those who share the same nature should not be deprived of the same benefits, especially that benefit which is grafted in that nature. Should we feel overburdened at satisfying not only our brothers' and sisters' just needs but also their pleasures, let us restrain our own if we do not want to be transgressors. We can be as indulgent as we like for ourselves providing we remember our neighbor has the same rights.

O fellow traveler, the law of life and order imposes on you the restraint of temperance lest you follow after your wanton desires and perish, lest you use nature's gifts to serve through wantonness the enemy of the soul. Would it not be more just and honorable to share them with your neighbor, your fellow, than with your enemy? If, faithful to the wise one's counsel, you turn away from sensual delights and content yourself with the teaching of the apostle [Paul] on food and clothing, you will soon be able to guard your love against "carnal desires which war against the soul." And I think you will not find it a burden to share with those of your nature that which you have withheld from the enemy of your soul. Your love will be sober and just when you do not refuse your brother and sister that which they need of what you have denied yourself in pleasure. Thus carnal love becomes social when it is extended to others.

What would you do if, while helping out your neighbor, you find yourself lacking what is necessary for your life? What else can you do than to pray with all confidence to him "who gives abundantly and bears no grudges, who opens his hand and fills with blessings every living being"? There is no doubt that he will assist us willingly in time of need since he helps us so often in time of plenty. It is written: "Seek first the kingdom of God and his justice, and the rest will be added thereto." Without being asked he promises to give what is necessary to us who withhold from ourselves what we do not need and love our neighbor. This is to seek the kingdom of God and implore his aid against the tyranny of sin, to prefer the yoke of chastity and sobriety rather than let sin reign in your mortal body. And again, it is only right to share nature's gifts with those who share that nature with you.

Nevertheless, in order to love one's neighbor with perfect justice, one must have regard to God. In other words, how can one love one's neighbor with purity if one does not love that neighbor in God? But it is impossible to love in God when one does not love God. It is necessary therefore to love God first, then one can love one's neighbor in God. Thus God makes himself lovable and creates whatever else is good. He does it this way. He who made nature protects it, for nature was created in a way that it must have its Creator as protector. The world could not subsist without him to whom it owes its very existence. No rational creature may ignore this fact concerning itself or dare lay claim through pride to benefits due the Creator. Therefore, the same Creator wills by a deep and salutary counsel that we be disciplined by tribulations, so that when we fail and God comes to our help we who are saved by God will render God the honor due him. It is written: "Call to me in the day of sorrow, I will deliver you and you shall honor me." In this way, we who are animal and carnal and know how to love only ourselves, start loving God for our own benefit. Because we learn from frequent experience that we can do everything that is good for ourselves in God and that without God we can do nothing good.

The second step of love:
We love God for our own sake

We therefore love God, but for our own sake and not yet for God's sake. Nevertheless, it is a matter of prudence to know what you can do by yourself and what you can do with God's help to keep from offending him who keeps you free from sin. If our tribulations, however, grow in frequency, and as a result we frequently turn to God and are frequently freed by God, must we not end, even though we had a heart of stone in a breast of iron, by realizing that it is God's grace that frees us, and come to love God not only for our own sake but because of who he is?

The third step of love: We love God because of who he is

Our frequent needs oblige us to invoke God more often and approach him more frequently. This intimacy moves us to taste and to discover how sweet the Lord is. Tasting God's sweetness entices us more to pure love than does the urgency of our own needs. Hence the example of the Samaritans who said to the woman who had told them the Lord was present: "We believe now not on account of what you said, for we have heard him and we know he is truly the Savior of the world." We walk in their footsteps when we say to our flesh, "Now we love God not because of your needs, for we have tasted and know how sweet the Lord is." The needs of the flesh are a kind of speech, proclaiming in transports of joy the good things experienced.

When we feel this way we will not have trouble in fulfilling the commandment to love our neighbor. We love God truthfully and so love what is God's. We love purely and we do not find it hard to obey a pure commandment, purifying the heart, as it is written, in the obedience of love. We love with justice and freely embrace the just commandment. This love is pleasing because it is free. It is chaste because it does not consist of spoken words but of deed and truth. It is just because it renders what is received. Whoever loves this way loves the way we are loved, seeking in turn not what is our own but what belongs to Christ, the same way Christ sought not what was his but what was ours, or rather, ourselves. He so loves who says: "Confess to the Lord for he is good." One who confesses to the Lord, not because the Lord is good to him or her but because the Lord is good, truly loves God for God's sake and not for one's own benefit. That one does not love in the way of the one of whom it is said: "That one will praise you when you do him or her favors." This is the third step of love: in it God is loved because of who he is.

The fourth step of love:
We love ourselves for God's sake

Happy the one who has attained the fourth degree of love. That one no longer loves self except for God. "O God, your justice is like the mountains of God." This love is a mountain, God's towering peak. Truly, indeed, it is the fat fertile mountain. "Who will climb the mountain of the Lord?" "Who will give me the wings of a dove, that I may fly away to find rest?" This place is made peaceful, a dwelling-place in Sion. "Alas for me, my exile has been lengthened." When will flesh and blood, this vessel of clay, this earthly dwelling, understand the fact? When will this sort of affection be felt that, inebriated with divine love, the mind may forget itself and become in its own eyes like a broken dish, hastening toward God and clinging to him, becoming one with him in spirit, saying: "My flesh and my heart have wasted away, O God of my heart, O God, my share for eternity." I would say that person is blessed and holy to whom it is given to experience something of this sort, so rare in life, even if it be but once and for the space of a moment. To lose yourself, as if you no longer existed, to cease completely to experience yourself, to reduce yourself to nothing, is not a human sentiment but a divine experience. If any mortal, suddenly rapt, as has been said, for a moment is admitted to this, immediately the world of sin envies that one. The evil of the day disturbs such a person, the mortal body weighs such a one down, the needs of the flesh bother, the weakness of corruption offers no support. And sometimes with greater violence than from these, charity toward the brothers and sisters recalls us. Alas, we have to come back to ourselves to descend again into our being and wretchedly cry out: "Lord, I suffer violence," adding, "Unhappy person that I am, who will free me from this body doomed to death?"

All the same, since scripture says God made everything for his own purpose, the day must come when the work will conform to and agree with its Maker. It is therefore necessary for our souls to reach a similar state. Then, just as God willed everything to exist for himself, so we wish that ourselves and other beings have been and are only for his will alone, not for our pleasure. The satisfaction of our wants, chance happiness, delights us less than to see his will done in us and for us, which we implore every day in prayer saying: "Your will be done on earth as it is in heaven."

O pure and sacred love! O sweet and pleasant affection! O pure and sinless intention of the will, all the more sinless and pure since it frees us from the stain of selfish vanity, all the more sweet and pleasant, for all that is found in it is divine. It is deifying to go through such an experience. As a drop of water seems to disappear completely in a big quantity of wine, even assuming the wine's taste and color, just as red, molten iron becomes so much like fire it seems to lose its primary state, just as the air on a sunny day seems transformed into sunshine instead of being lit up, so it is necessary for the saints that all human feelings melt in a mysterious way and flow into the will of God. Otherwise, how will God be all in all if something human survives in us? No doubt, the substance remains, though under another form, another glory, another power. When will this happen? Who will see it? Who will possess it? "When shall I come and when shall I appear in God's presence?" O my Lord, my God, "my heart said to you: My face has sought you, Lord, I will seek your face." Do you think I shall see your holy temple?

I do not think that this can take place for sure until the word is fulfilled: "You will love the Lord your God with all your heart, all your soul, and all your strength," until the heart does not have to think of the body, and the soul no longer has to give it life and feeling, as is the case in this life. Freed from this bother, its strength is established in the power of God. For it is impossible to assemble all these and turn them toward God's face as long as the care of this weak and wretched body keeps one busy to the point of distraction. Hence it is in a spiritual and immortal body, calm and pleasant, subject to the spirit in everything, that the soul hopes to attain the fourth step of love, or rather, to be possessed by it. For it is in God's hands to give it to whom he wishes. It is not obtained by human efforts. I mean we will easily reach the highest step of love when we will no longer be held back by any desire of the flesh nor upset by troubles, as we hasten with the greatest speed and desire toward the joy of the Lord.

Consequently, until death is swallowed up in victory, until eternal light invades from all sides the limits of night and takes possession to the extent that heavenly glory shines in our bodies, we cannot set ourselves aside and pass into God. We are still attached to our bodies, if not by life and feeling, certainly by a natural affection, so that they do not wish nor are able to realize their consummation without them. This rapture of the soul, which is its most perfect and highest state, cannot, therefore, take place before the resurrection of the body. Because the spirit, if it could reach perfection without the body, would no longer desire to be united to the flesh. For, indeed, the body is not deposed or resumed without profit for the soul.

To be brief, "The death of his saints is precious in the sight of the Lord. " If death is precious, what must life be, especially that life? Do not be surprised if the glorified body seems to give the spirit something, for it was a real help when we were sick and mortal. How true that text is which says that all things turn to the good of those who love God. The sick, the dead and the resurrected body is a help to the soul who loves God; the first for the fruits of penance, the second for repose, and the third for consummation. Truly the soul does not want to be perfected without that from whose good services it feels it has benefited in every way.

The flesh is clearly a good and faithful partner for a good spirit. It helps if it is burdened; it relieves if it does not help. It surely benefits and is by no means a burden. The first state is that of fruitful labor; the second is restful but by no means tiresome; the third is above all glorious. Listen to the Bridegroom in the Song of Songs inviting us to this triple progress: "Eat, friends, and drink, be inebriated, dearest ones." He calls to those working in the body to eat; he invites those who have set aside their bodies to drink, and he impels those who have resumed their bodies to inebriate themselves, calling them his dearest ones as if they were filled with charity. There is a difference between those who are simply called friends, who sigh under the weight of the flesh, who are held to be dear for their charity, and those who are free from the bonds of the flesh who are all the more dear because they are more ready and free to love. More than the other two, these last ones are called dearest and are so. Receiving a second garment they are in their resumed and glorified bodies. They are that much more freely and willingly borne toward God's love because nothing at all remains to solicit them or hold them back. Neither of the first two states can claim this, because in the first state the body is endured with distress; in the second state it is hoped for as for something missing.

In the first state, therefore, the faithful soul eats its bread, but alas, in the sweat of its brow. While in the flesh it moves by faith which necessarily acts through charity, for if it does not act, it dies. Moreover, according to our Savior, this work is food: "My food is to do the will of my Father." Afterward, having cast off its flesh, the soul no longer feeds on the bread of sorrow. Having eaten, it is allowed to drink of the wine of love, not pure wine, for it is written of the bride in the Song of Songs: "I drank my wine mixed with milk." The soul mixes the divine love with the tenderness of that natural affection by which it desired to have its body back, a glorified body. The soul, therefore, glows already with the warmth of charity's wine, but not to the stage of intoxication, for the milk moderates its strength. Intoxication disturbs the mind and makes it wholly forgetful of itself, but the soul which still thinks of the resurrection of its own body had not forgotten itself completely. For the rest, after finding the only thing needed, what is there to prevent the soul from taking leave of itself and passing into God entirely, ceasing all the more to be like itself as it becomes more and more like God? Only then the soul is allowed to drink wisdom's pure wine of which it is said: "How good is my cup, it inebriates me!" Why wonder if the soul is inebriated by the riches of the Lord's dwelling when, free from worldly cares, it can drink pure fresh wine with Christ in his Father's house.

At last here is that sober intoxication of truth, not from overdrinking, not reeking with wine but burning for God. From this, then, that fourth degree of love is possessed forever when God alone is loved in the highest way. For now we do not love ourselves except for his sake, that he may be the reward of those who love him, the eternal recompense of those who love him forever.

(*On Loving God* 30ff)

A summation

Love is the excellent food. Its place is in the middle of the dish of Solomon, the dish which diffuses the mingled odor of virtues, fragrant as all the powders of the perfumer. It fills the hungry and gives joy to those being filled. On this dish we find peace and patience and longanimity and joy in the Holy Spirit, and any other kind of virtue, any other fruit of wisdom you can think of. Humility has it own contribution to the banquet and graces the dish with the bread of sorrow and the wine of compunction. Truth offers these first to beginners, saying, "Rise up after you have been seated, you who eat the bread of sorrow." Contemplation then brings its offering of solid bread of wisdom made of the finest wheat and the wine which gladdens the human heart, to which Truth calls the perfect with the words: "Eat, my friends, and drink; be inebriated, my dearest ones." Truth does not fail to make provision for the less perfect. "Love is placed in the middle for the daughters of Jerusalem." These are the ones not yet able to take solid food, so Truth gives them love's milk instead of bread, and oil instead of wine. This portion is "in the middle" because beginners could not yet relish it, being too much afraid. The perfect find it insufficient now that they have plenty of the sweet food of contemplation. Beginners are not able to enjoy the sweetness of milk until they have been purged by the bitter draughts of fear. It must cleanse them of the infection of carnal pleasures. The perfect now turn from milk since they have had a glorious foretaste of the feast of glory. Only those in the middle, those who are growing, who are still delicate, are content with the sweet milk foods of charity.

The first food, then, is humility: bitter but medicinal; the second is charity: sweet and soothing; the third is contemplation: solid and strength-giving.

(The Steps of Humility and Pride 4f)

A Twosome

Saint Bernard has built his ladders, one atop the other, reaching to the very heights of the heavenly life, to the inner life of the most Holy Trinity. His presentation is simple enough; the steps are practical and concise. But what about the climber? And where does he or she get the will to climb? These are precisely the questions that the Abbot of Clairvaux now studies with his usual clarity.

His essay on *Grace and Free Choice* was addressed to his friend, William of Saint Thierry. It opens with the report of a dialogue which may well represent an exchange that actually took place between the two friends. Together they had studied the way of love; now they were concerned about the lover.

Love of its very nature is free, it is a free choice. And yet the Lord has said: "Without me you can do nothing." How can we do it with him, dependent on him, and yet choose freely? Later theologians will struggle long and hard with this question as had some earlier ones. Bernard is content to leave the mystery but to clearly affirm the respective roles and responsibilities. His is a practical answer: Grace does the whole work and so does free choice. But he gives this qualification: Whereas the whole is a work done *in* free choice, so the whole is a work *of* grace. Without the two the work cannot be done: the one as the operative principle, the other as the object in which it is accomplished. God is the author of grace; none but God can give it, none but free choice can receive it. To consent is to be saved. Ours is to receive God's grace and move with it.

In developing this teaching, Bernard gives us many distinctions and examples which help us to understand more fully the inner workings of our human life. The more we know ourselves, the better and more easily we can cooperate with grace in our ascent to God and to the fullness to which we are called by our very nature.

In the course of this essay, Bernard again affirms the preeminence of the contemplative dimension of our lives.

Grace and Free Will

Once, in conversation, I happened to refer to my experience of God's grace, how I recognized myself as being impelled to good by its prevenient action, felt myself being borne along by it and helped, with its help, to find perfection.

"What part do you play, then," asked a bystander, "or what reward or prize do you hope for, if it is all God's work?"

"What do you think yourself?" I replied.

"Glorify God," he said, "who freely went before you, aroused and set you moving; and then live a worthy life to prove your gratitude for kindnesses received and your suitability for receiving more."

"That is sound advice," I observed, "if only you could give me the means to carry it out. Indeed, it is easier to know what one ought to do than to do it. For it is one thing to lead the blind and another to provide a vehicle for the weary. Not every guide supplies the traveler with the food for the journey. The one who sets him in the right direction gives him one thing; the one who provides him with food to keep him from fainting on the way, another. So, too, not every teacher is automatically a communicator of the good he teaches. Hence, I stand in need of two things: instruction and help. You, friend, certainly give fine instruction for my ignorance but, unless the apostle [Paul] be mistaken, it is the Spirit who helps our weakness. Indeed, the One who advises me by means of your words must assist me also through his Spirit, so that I may be able to do as you advise. For it is already due partly to his assistance that I can will what is right, although I cannot do it. But I would have no grounds for believing that I would some day manage to do it, were it not that he who has given me to will shall also enable me to accomplish on account of my good will."

"Where then," said he, "are our merits or where our hope?"

"Listen," I replied. "He saves us not because of deeds done by us in righteousness but in virtue of his own mercy. What? Did you imagine that you create your own merits, that you can be saved by your own righteousness, you who cannot even say 'Jesus is Lord' without the Holy Spirit? Or have you forgotten the words: 'Without me you can do nothing,' and 'It depends not on the one running, nor the one willing, but on God who has mercy'?"

You ask: "What part, then, does free choice play?"

I shall answer you in a word: It is saved. Take away free choice and there is nothing to be saved. Take away grace and there is no means of saving. Without the two combined this work cannot be done: the One as operative principle, the other as object toward which or in which it is accomplished. God is the author of salvation, the free choice is only capable of receiving it. What, therefore, is given by God alone and to free choice alone, cannot any more happen without the recipient's consent than without the Bestower's grace. Consequently, free choice is said to co-operate with operating grace in its act of consent or, in other words, in its process of being saved. For to consent is to be saved.

That is why the animal spirit does not receive this salvation: It lacks the power of voluntary consent by which it might tranquilly submit to a saving God whether by acquiescing in his commands or by believing his promises or by giving thanks for his benefits.

Voluntary consent is a self-determining power of the soul. Its action is neither forced nor extorted. It stems from the will and not from necessity, denying or giving itself on no issue except by way of the will. But if it is compelled in spite of itself, then there is violent, not voluntary, consent. Where the will is absent, so is consent, for only what is voluntary may be called consent. Hence, where you have consent, there also is the will. But where the will is, there is freedom. And this is what I mean by the term "free choice."

(*Grace and Free Choice* 1f)

Three Kinds of Freedom

There are three kinds of freedom, as they occur to us: freedom from sin, freedom from sorrow, and freedom from necessity. The last belongs to our natural condition, the first we are restored to by grace, and the second is reserved for us in our homeland.

The first freedom might be termed freedom of nature, the second of grace, and the third of life or glory. At first we were created with free will and voluntary freedom, a creature noble in God's eyes. Secondly, we are re-formed in innocence, a new creature in Christ. And thirdly, we are raised up to glory, a perfect creation in the Spirit. The first freedom is thus a title of considerable honor, the second of even greater power, and the last of total happiness. By the first we have the advantage over other living things, by the second over the flesh, by the third we overcome death itself. Or, to express it another way, in the first God put under our feet sheep and oxen and the beasts of the field. In the second he laid out flat and crushed under our feet those spiritual beasts of the world of whom it is said: "Do not deliver the souls of those who trust in you to the wild beasts." Finally, by the last, in our more perfect submission to ourselves through victory over corruption and death — when death shall be, last of all, destroyed — we will pass over into the glorious freedom of the children of God. By this freedom Christ will set us free when he delivers us as a kingdom to God the Father. Of this last freedom, I think, and also of the one we have called freedom from sin, he said to the Jews: "If the Son makes you free, you will be free indeed." He meant that even free choice stands in need of a liberator. A liberator, of course, who would set it free not from necessity, which was quite unknown to it since this pertains to the will, but rather from sin, into which it had fallen both freely and willingly, and also from the penalty of sin, which it carelessly incurred and has unwillingly borne. From these two evils free choice was quite unable to extricate itself except through him who alone of all humans was made free among the dead, free, that is, from sin in the midst of sinners.

Christ alone, among the sons of Adam, was free from sin.

(*Grace and Free Choice* 7f)

Freedom from necessity

Freedom from necessity belongs alike to God and to every rational creature, good or bad. Neither by sin nor by suffering is it lost or lessened; nor is it greater in the just person than in the sinner, nor fuller in the angel than in the human. The consent of the human will, which is directed by grace toward the good, makes the person freely good and, in the good, free by the fact that it is voluntarily given and not unwillingly extorted. In the same way, when the consent willingly goes toward the bad it makes the person nonetheless free and spontaneous in doing evil. The person is not forced to be evil by some other cause. That one simply chooses to be so, led by his or her own will. And just as the angels in heaven and even God himself remain freely good, that is, they remain good by their own will and not from any extrinsic necessity, so the devil freely opts for evil and persists in it not by coercion from without but of his own free choice. Freedom of will thus continues to exist, even where the mind is captive, as fully in the bad as in the good, yet more orderly in the good. It is complete in its own way in the creature as in the Creator, yet more powerfully in the Creator.

When a person complains saying: "I *wish* I could have a good will but I just can't manage it," this in no way argues against the freedom of which we have been speaking, as if the will thus suffered violence or were subject to necessity. Rather, that person is witnessing to the fact that he or she lacks that freedom which is called freedom from sin. Because those who want to have a good will prove thereby that they have a will, since their desire is aimed at good only through their will. And if they find themselves unable to have a good will whereas they really want to, then this is because they feel freedom is lacking to them, freedom namely from sin, by which it pains them that their will is oppressed, though it is not suppressed. Indeed it is more than likely that, since they want to have a good will, they do to some extent have it. What they want is good, and they could hardly want good otherwise than by means of a good will, just as they could want evil only by a bad will. When we desire good then our will is good; when we desire evil, our will is evil. In both cases there is will and in both freedom. Necessity yields to will. But if we are unable to do what we will, we feel that freedom itself is somehow captive to sin or misery, not that it is lost.

In my opinion, therefore, free choice takes its name from that freedom alone by which the will is free either to judge itself good, if it has consented to good, or bad, if to evil. Only by willing, in fact, can it feel itself to consent to either.

Freedom from sin might, perhaps, more fittingly be called free counsel and freedom from sorrow, free pleasure rather than free choice.

Choice is an act of judgment. But even as it belongs to judgment to distinguish between what is lawful and what is not, so it belongs to counsel to examine what is expedient and what is not, and to pleasure to experience what is pleasant and what is not.

(*Grace and Free Choice* 9ff)

"Your kingdom come"

One thing is certain: we *shall* possess free counsel and free pleasure when, by God's mercy, we shall obtain what we pray for: "Your will be done on earth as it is in heaven." This shall come to pass, as has been said, when that which appears common to every rational creature, namely, a choice which is free from necessity, shall be in the elect of the human race also, as it is already in the holy angels: secure from sin and safe from sorrow. This happy experience of these three freedoms will prove what is the good, acceptable and perfect will of God. In the meantime, this is not yet so. In its full measure, we have only freedom of choice. Freedom of counsel is possessed only in part, and that only in the few spiritual ones among us who have crucified their flesh with its passions and desires so that sin no longer reigns in their mortal bodies. Now it is freedom of counsel which brings it about that sin does not so reign. That it still has some small hold is due to the fact that free choice is still captive. "But when the perfect comes, then the imperfect will pass away." This means: When freedom of counsel shall have been fully achieved, the judgment's shackles shall also fall away.

And that is what we daily ask in prayer when we say to God: "Your kingdom come." This kingdom is not yet wholly established among us. But it comes closer by degrees each day, and daily it gradually extends its bounds. It does so in those whose interior self, with the help of God, is renewed from day to day. In the measure that grace's kingdom is extended, sin's power is weakened. It is a process which is still unfinished because of this perishable body which weighs down the soul, and because of the needy condition of this earthly dwelling which burdens the mind full of thoughts. Even those who appear more perfect in this mortal state have to acknowledge that "in many things we all offend" and "if we say we have no sin, we deceive ourselves and the truth is not in us." That is why they pray without ceasing: "Your kingdom come." But this will not be fully accomplished even in them until sin not only has no further sway over their perishable bodies but no longer is at all, nor can be, in a body that is immortal.

(*Grace and Free Choice* 12f)

Freedom of pleasure

What shall we say about freedom of pleasure in this present evil age? The day's own trouble is scarcely sufficient for the day; every creature groans and is in labor until now, subjected as it is to futility not of its own will; the life of a person is a hard service upon the earth; even the spiritual ones who have already received the first fruits of the Spirit groan inwardly, awaiting the redemption of their bodies. Can there really be room in such a situation for this type of freedom? What is left free for our good pleasure, I ask, where every square inch seems to be taken up by sorrow? Indeed, here not even innocence or righteousness are immune from sorrow (any more than they are from sin), where the just one cries out: "Wretched person that I am! Who will deliver me from this body of death?" And again: "My tears have been my food day and night." Where night follows day and day night in one rhythm of sorrow, there is no moment's room for real pleasure. And then, all those who desire to live a godly life in Christ will suffer more persecution, since judgment begins with the household of God, as he commanded, saying: "Begin with mine."

Yet, though virtue is not immune from sorrow, perhaps vice is. Can it at times enjoy pleasure in some part, avoiding misery? No! For those who rejoice in doing evil and delight in the worst sort of things, imitate the wild laughter of the mad. No sorrow is more truly sorrow than false joy. The more a thing wears the guise of happiness in this world, the more is it misery. As the Wise One says: "It is better to go to the house of mourning than to go to the house of feasting."

(Grace and Free Choice 13)

Corporal joy

A certain pleasure is to be found in goods of the body, namely, in eating, drinking, warm clothing, and in the other things that pamper and adorn the body. But do even these escape affliction? Bread is fine, but to one who is hungry. Drink is delightful, but to the thirsty. To the sated food and drink are a burden, not a joy. Once hunger has been eased, bread will mean little to you. Thirst slaked, even the most limpid font will no more attract you than a swamp. Only those who are hot seek the shade. Only the cold or those in darkness hail the sun. None of these things pleases without the prick of necessity. Take this away and at once the pleasure which seemed to form part of them yields to tedium and distaste.

It must therefore be admitted here again that everything belonging to the present life involves suffering. The only mitigating factor is that in the midst of the relentless hardships which go with our more difficult undertakings, lighter tasks come as a sort of relaxation. In a given time and situation, while heavy and light alternate, the experience of the light seems to provide an interlude to sorrow, as when sometimes we think it a joy when we pass out of the doldrums of nerve-racking trials into worries of a milder kind.

(*Grace and Free Choice* 14)

The Joy of Contemplation

But what of those who at times, being caught up in the Spirit through the ecstasy of contemplation, become capable of savoring something of the sweetness of heavenly bliss? Do these attain to freedom from sorrow as often as this happens to them? Yes, indeed. Even in this present life, those who with Mary have chosen the better part — which shall not be taken away from them — enjoy freedom of pleasure; rarely, however, and fleetingly. This pleasure is undeniable. For those who now possess that which shall never be taken away, plainly experience what is to come. In a word, happiness. And since happiness and sorrow are incompatible, as often as these participate through the Spirit in the former they cease to feel the latter. Hence, on this earth, contemplatives alone can in some way enjoy freedom of pleasure, though only in part, in a sufficiently modest part, and on very rare occasions.

(*Grace and Free Choice* 15)

Grace is Necessary

I think it has been clearly shown that even freedom of choice is to some extent held captive as long as it is unaccompanied or imperfectly accompanied by the two other freedoms. From no other cause arises this frailty of ours of which the apostle [Paul] speaks: "So that the things you would not, these you do." To will, indeed, lies in our power as a result of free choice but not to carry out what we will. I am not saying to will the good or to will the bad, but simply to will. For to will the good indicates an achievement, and to will the bad a defect. Simply to will denotes the subject itself, which does either the achieving or the failing. To this subject, however, creating grace gives existence. Saving grace gives it the achievement. But when it fails, it is to blame for its own failure. Free choice, accordingly, constitutes us willers; grace, willers of the good. Because of our willing faculty, we are able to will; because of grace, we are able to will the good. Just as to simply fear is one thing and to fear God another, to love is one thing and to love God another. For to fear and to love on their own signify affections, but coupled with the additional word "God" they signify virtues. So, too, to will is one thing and to will the good another.

Mere affections live naturally in us, as if they were finding their source in us, but those additional acts are of grace.

Nothing is made perfect in us except that which creation has given and grace sets in order, so virtues are nothing else than ordered affections.

That is why the Bride in the Song of Songs says: "Set charity in order in me."

Freedom of choice continues to operate in us so the basis for merit remains. Meritedly then, when we are bad we are punished for the bad we did of our own free choice, and we are glorified for the good which could not have been without a similar decision of our will. It is our own will that enslaves us to the devil, not his power. Whereas it is God's grace which subjects us to God, not our own will. Our will, created good (as must be granted) by the good God, shall nevertheless be perfect only when perfectly subjected to its Creator. This does not mean that we ascribe to it its own perfection and to God only its creation, since to be perfect is far more than to be made. Attributing to God of what is less and to ourselves of what is more surely stands condemned in the very statement. Finally, the apostle [Paul], feeling what he was by nature and what he hoped to be by grace, said: "I can will what is right but I cannot do it." He realized that to will was possible to him as a result of free choice, but that for this will to be perfect he stood in need of grace. For if to will what is evil is a defect of the willing faculty, then undoubtedly to will what is good marks a growth in this same faculty. And to measure up to every good thing that we will is its perfection.

In order, then, that our willing derived from our free choice may be perfect, we need a twofold gift of grace: true wisdom, which means the turning of the will to good, and full power, which means its confirmation in good.

From the first moment of its existence, the will posseses in itself a twofold goodness: The general one, from the very fact of creation, for by a good God only good could be created — "God saw everything he had made and behold, they were very good"; and the special one, arising from its freedom of choice, by which it was made in the image of him who created it. And if to these two goods we add a third, conversion to the Creator, then the will may rightly be regarded as perfectly good: good, that is, as part of a good creation; better within its own sphere of action; best in its orientation. This latter implies the total conversion of the will to God and its wholehearted, voluntary and devoted subjection.

(*Grace and Free Choice* 19)

Sin

Three freedoms the first man received. By abusing the one called freedom of choice, he deprived himself of the others. He abused it, in that what he had received for his glory he turned to his shame as the scripture says: "Man, when he was in honor did not understand; he became like the senseless beasts."

Among all living beings, to the human person alone was given the ability to sin as part of his prerogative of free choice. But we were given it not that we might sin, but that we might appear the more glorious did we not sin when we were capable of doing so. What in fact could afford us greater glory than that scripture's words be spoken of us: "Who is the one and we shall praise that one?" Why such praise? "For that one has done wonderful things in life." What kind of things? "That person had the power to transgress and did not transgress and to do evil and did not do it." This honor the first man kept as long as he was sinless, but once he sinned he lost it. He sinned because he was free to sin, and free from no other source than his own freedom of choice, which bore within it the possibility of sinning. No failure this of the Bestower but rather of the abuser, who made over to the service of sin that faculty he had received for the glory of not sinning. For though the root of his sin lay in the ability received, yet he sinned not because he was able to but because he willed to. So it was that when the devil and his angels rebelled, others of their company refused to do so not because they could not but because they would not.

The sinner's fall, therefore, was not due to the gift of being able to but to the vice of willing to. However, if he fell by the power of his will, this does not mean that he was equally free to rise again by the same power. The ability to remain standing lest he fall was indeed given to his will but not to get up again once he fell. It is not as easy to climb out of a pit as to fall into one. By his will alone, man fell into the pit of sin, but he cannot climb out of his will alone, since now even if he wishes he cannot not sin.

Does the fact that we cannot sin then put an end to free choice? No. But we lost free counsel by which previously we had enjoyed the ability not to sin.

And this is where Christ comes in. In him we possess the necessary power of God and wisdom of God. Christ, inasmuch as he is wisdom, pours back into us true wisdom and so restores to us our free counsel and, inasmuch as he is power, renews our full power and restores to us our free pleasure.

Here below, we must learn from our freedom of counsel not to abuse free choice so that one day we may be able to fully enjoy freedom of pleasure. Thus we are repairing the image of God in us, and the way is being paved, by grace, for the retrieving of that former honor which we forfeited by sin. Happy then will be the person who shall deserve to hear said of him or her: "Who is this and we shall praise this one. For this one has done wonderful things in life. That person had the power to transgress and did not transgress, to do evil and did not do it."

(Grace and Free Choice 22ff)

The image and likeness of the Creator

I believe that in these three freedoms there is contained the image and likeness of the Creator in which we were made. In freedom of choice lies the image, and in the other two is contained a certain twofold likeness. Maybe the reason why free choice alone suffers no lessening or falling away is that in it, more than in the others, there seems to be imprinted some substantial image of the eternal and immutable divinity.

Although it had a beginning, free choice knows no end, nor has it experience either of increase through righteousness or glory or decrease through sin or sorrow. What could be more like eternity without actually being eternity? Now, in the other two freedoms, liable not only to partial diminution but even to total loss, one sees added to the image a certain more accidental likeness of the power and wisdom. By a fault we lost them. By grace we recovered them. And daily, each of us in varying degrees, either advances in them or falls away. They may be even irreparably lost. And they can be so possessed that they cannot in any way be lost nor diminished.

(*Grace and Free Choice* 28f)

Through Christ the likeness is restored in us

In this present world the proper likeness could not be found. Even the image would still have lain stained and deformed had not that woman of the gospel lit her lamp (had Wisdom not appeared in the flesh), swept the house (of the vices), and searched carefully for her lost coin (her image). Its original luster gone, covered over with the coating of transgression, the image lay buried, as it were, in the dust. She found it, wiped it clean, and rescued it from the "region of unlikeness." Then she refashioned it to its erstwhile beauty and made it like the saints in glory. Some day she will make it quite conformable to herself. On that day the words of scripture will be fulfilled: "We know that when he appears we shall be like him, for we shall see him as he is." To whom, in fact, could this work be better suited than to the Son of God who, being the splendor and the figure of the Father's substance, upholding all things by his word, was well qualified for it. He was able to reform what was deformed, strengthen what was weak and, dispelling with the splendor of his own figure the shadows of sin, make us wise. By the might of his word he lent us strength against the tyranny of the demons.

(*Grace and Free Choice* 32)

Free choice should govern the body

Free choice should try to govern its body as wisdom does the world. It should reach mightily from end to end, strongly commanding each sense and each member that it will not suffer sin to reign in its mortal body. It will not give its members over as instruments of wickedness but rather to serve justice. And so we will no longer be servants of sin, since we will not commit sin. Further, set free from sin, we can now begin to recover our freedom of counsel and vindicate our dignity. We can reestablish in ourselves a worthy likeness to the divine image, in fact, we can completely restore our former loveliness. But let us take care to do this no less gently than mightily, not reluctantly or under compulsion, but with prompt and ready will, for this is the beginning, not the fullness of wisdom. This makes the offering acceptable, since "God loves a cheerful giver." In this way we will be imitating wisdom in all we do, mightily resisting vices and being gently at rest with our own conscience.

We cannot achieve these things, however, without the help of him by whose example we are spurred on to desire them. With his help, and by it, we ourselves are conformed and transformed into the same image from glory to glory, as by the Spirit of the Lord. But if by the Spirit of the Lord, then hardly by free choice. Let no one imagine, therefore, that free choice is so called because it affects good and evil with equal power or facility. It was indeed able to fall of itself, but it can rise up again only through the Spirit of the Lord.

(*Grace and Free Choice* 34f)

Grace and free choice in the work of salvation

Are we to say, then, that the entire function and the sole merit of free choice lies in its consent? Assuredly. Not that this consent in which all merit consists is its own doing, since we are unable even to think anything of ourselves, which is less than consent.

These words are not mine but the apostle's, who attributes everything susceptible of good to God and not to his own choosing power: thinking, willing and accomplishing for his good pleasure. If, then, God works these three things in us, namely thinking, willing and accomplishing the good, the first he does without us, the second with us, and the third through us. By suggesting the good thought, he goes one first step ahead of us. By also bringing about the change of our ill will, he joins it to himself by its consent. And by supplying consent with the faculty and ability, the Operator within makes his appearance outwardly through the external work that we perform. Of ourselves we cannot, of course, take that first step. But he who can find no one who is good, can save no one without his first stepping into the lead. There can be no doubt, therefore, that the beginning action rests with God and is enacted neither through us nor with us. The consent and the work, however, though not originating from us nevertheless are not without us.

We must therefore be careful, whenever we feel these things happening invisibly within us and with us, not to attribute them to our own weak will nor to any necessity on the part of God — for there is none — but to that grace alone of which he is full. It is this grace which arouses free choice when it sows the seed of the good thought, which heals free choice by changing its disposition, which strengthens it so as to lead it to action, and which saves it from experiencing a fall. Grace so cooperates with free choice, however, that only in the first movement does it go a step ahead of it. In the others it accompanies it. Indeed, grace's whole aim in taking the step ahead is that from then on free choice may co-operate with it. What was begun by grace alone is completed by grace and free choice together in such a way that they contribute to each new achievement not singly but jointly, not by turn but simultaneously. It is not as if grace did one half of the work and free choice the other. Each does the whole work according to its own proper contribution. Grace does the whole work and so does free choice with this one qualification: Whereas the whole is done *in* free choice, the whole is done *of* grace.

We trust the reader is pleased to find that we have never strayed from the meaning of the apostle [Paul], and that wherever our words may have wandered we found ourselves often returning to almost his very words. For what else does what we are saying amount to but, "So it depends not upon the human's will or exertion but on God's mercy." He does not say this as if it were possible for a person to will or to run in vain. What he means is that we who will and run should glory not in ourselves but in him from whom we received in the first place the power both to will and to run. In a word: "What have you that you did not receive?"

You are created, healed, saved. Which of these, O human, comes from you? Which is not impossible to free choice? You could neither create yourself, since you were not there to do so, nor when in sin could you restore yourself to grace, nor raise yourself from the dead. And this is to say nothing of those other good things which are either necessary to those who have been healed or laid up for those who are to be saved.

Those, therefore, who possess true wisdom acknowledge a threefold operation, not indeed of free choice, but of divine grace in free choice, or concerning it. The first is creation, the second reformation, and the third consummation. Created first in Christ unto freedom of will, by the second we are reformed through Christ unto the spirit of freedom. Lastly we reach fulfillment with Christ in eternity.

What had no existence had to be created by one who had; what was deformed had to be reformed through the Form [Christ, who was in the form of God]; the members can only be perfected with the Head. This will happen when we all shall have attained "to mature personhood, to the measure of the stature of the fullness of Christ." When Christ who is our life appears, we also shall appear with him in glory.

(*Grace and Free Choice* 46ff)

A Never Ending Romance

His *Sermons on the Song of Songs* are Bernard's masterpiece. He started writing them in 1136 and was in the midst of writing the eighty-sixth sermon when he died. They probably do represent talks he gave to his brothers in the chapterhouse of Clairvaux, but they are in fact literary works cast in the form of sermons and meant for a much wider audience, which they got. They represent the work and thought of a mature man at the pinnacle of his life, a man of great influence and lofty mystical experience.

Many find the sermons difficult to read, and this for a number of reasons. As he moves along commenting on the Song of Songs verse by verse, word by word, Bernard introduces into his spiritual teaching all sorts of extraneous matters. The one who is looking for spiritual teaching, as we are in this book, would prefer he might have kept to that and not included the political and ecclesial affairs, the theological controversies, the outbreaks of personal emotion and family affairs, etc. But I believe Bernard very deliberately included all of this as an important part of his teaching. We are all too apt to make the "spiritual life" a very particular part of our life, perhaps a rather esoteric part. No, the journey into Christ, in Christ, is woven into the very fabric of our lives. We do not have any "spiritual life." We are, like our Master and Lord, very incarnate. The only life we have is the very real everyday life that should be filled with family affairs, ecclesial activities, and political concerns. It is all of a piece.

We shouldn't be frightened by the term "mystical." Actually, Bernard rarely uses it, though writers use it a great deal in speaking about his life and teaching. The fact is that everyone of us at baptism receives the Holy Spirit and the gifts of the Spirit. The "mystical life" essentially is nothing other than the activity of the Spirit in our lives, when the Holy Spirit through the activity of the gifts brings us intuitions and experiences of God that are beyond those we can attain with our human reason and senses. God is God. He is beyond us. If we are going to really experience God, experience a loving relationship with him, we have to be ready to leave the limitations of our human reason behind and move into other realms of knowledge and experience. This is what Bernard is seeking to help us understand.

Precisely because what Bernard is talking about is beyond the thoughts and concepts of ordinary human reason, he has recourse to allegory and image. And because he is speaking of God and our relationship with God, where better could he find his images and allegories than in the inspired Word of God. This invitation into the domain of poetry and beyond may be very unfamiliar to the pragmatic and the prosaic. But a willingness to let go of the programmatic that we feel comfortable with because we feel we can control it, is perhaps for us the first step toward a willingness to let go and let God — to let go of our rational control and let the Spirit have space to open up new realms to us through the gifts, realms that will begin to satisfy those deepest longings, that we usually have not even dared to admit exist in us, because they seem to be unfulfillable.

Come, let Bernard sing to you for a bit, inspired by the divine Song of Songs.

In the Weave of Life

Rightly it is called the Song of Songs. Grace alone can teach it, it cannot be learned except by experience. It is for the experienced, therefore, to recognize it and for others to burn with the desire, not so much of knowing as of experiencing it, since this canticle is not a noise made by the mouth but a jubilation of heart, not a sound of the lips but a tumult of internal joys, not a symphony of voices but a harmony of wills. It is not heard outside for it does not sound externally. The singer alone can hear it and he to whom it is sung, namely the Bridegroom and the bride. For it is a nuptial song, celebrating the chaste and joyous embraces of loving hearts, the concord of minds and the union resulting from reciprocal affection.

(*On the Song of Songs* 1:11)

You have seen the way we must follow, the order of procedure. First we cast ourselves at his feet, we "kneel before the Lord, our maker," deploring the evil we have done. Then we reach out for the hand that will lift us up, that will steady our trembling knees. And finally, when we shall have obtained these favors through many prayers and tears, we humbly dare to raise our eyes to his mouth, so divinely beautiful, not merely to gaze upon, but — I say with fear and trembling — to receive his kiss; for Christ the Lord is a Spirit before our face. And we who are joined to him in a holy kiss become, at his good pleasure, one spirit with him.

(On the Song of Songs 3:5)

Even to me, miserable as I am, it has been given sometimes to sit at the feet of the Lord Jesus and to embrace with all devotion now one foot, now the other, insofar as his gracious mercy deigned to permit. But whenever, under the sting of my conscience, I lost sight of the divine mercy and clung a little too long to the foot of justice, immediately I became oppressed with an indescribable terror and a miserable confusion and, enveloped in the most horrible darkness, I could only cry tremblingly, "From out of the depths, who knows the power of your anger and who for fear of you can endure your wrath?" And if, leaving the foot of justice, I should chance to lay hold of that of mercy, I straightaway grew more tepid at prayer, more slothful at work, more ready for laughter, more imprudent in speech. In short, my whole being, body and soul, showed evidence of greater inconstancy. Therefore, taught by experience, no longer judgment alone or mercy alone but both "mercy and judgment, I will sing to you, O Lord."

(On the Song of Songs 6:9)

If you willingly share with us your brothers and sisters the gifts you have received from above, if you show yourself everywhere among us obliging, affectionate, graceful, obedient and humble, you also shall receive the testimony of all that you, too, are redolent with the best of ointments.

Yes, every one among you, my sisters and brothers, who not only supports with patience the corporal and spiritual infirmities of his brother and sister but, insofar as he is permitted and has power, assists them by kind services, comforts them by his words, and directs them by counsels or consoles the weak ones at least by fervent and incessant prayer — every such brother and sister, I say, exhales a good odor in their community and smells sweet with the best ointments.

(*On the Song of Songs* 12:5)

Those who are wise will see their lives as more like a reservoir than a canal. The canal simultaneously pours out what it receives; the reservoir retains the water till it is filled, then pours forth the overflow without loss to itself. They know that a curse is on those who allow their own property to degenerate. And if you think my opinion worthless then listen to one who is wiser than I. "Fools," said Solomon, "come out with all their feelings at once but the wise subdue and restrain them." Today there are many in the Church who act like canals, the reservoirs are far too rare. So urgent is the charity of those through whom the streams of heavenly doctrine flow to us that they want to pour it forth before they have been filled. They are more ready to speak than to listen, impatient to teach what they have not grasped, and full of presumption to govern others while they know not how to govern themselves.

I am convinced that no degree of charity that leads to salvation may be preferred to that suggested by the Wise One, "Have pity on your own soul, pleasing God." Listen to what a prudent and vigilant charity advises, "This does not mean that to give relief to others you ought to make things difficult for yourselves. It is a question of balancing."

The reservoir resembles the fountain that runs to form a stream or spreads to form a pool only when its own waters are brimming over. The reservoir is not ashamed to be no more lavish than the spring that fills it. He who is the primal Fountain of Life, full in himself and filled with himself, gushed forth and danced into the secret places of the heavens about him, to fill them all with his favors. And having endowed these remotest heights and recesses, he burst upon our earth, saving humans and beasts through his munificence, multiplying his mercies everywhere. When he had first filled up the secret places, his teeming mercies billowed over. They poured upon the earth and drenched it, to multiply its riches. You must imitate this process. First be filled and then control the outpouring. The charity that is benign and prudent does not flow outward until it abounds within.

(*On the Song of Songs* 13:3-4)

I wish to remind you now of the principles necessary for our salvation and how to apply them, the truths that must be infused into us and their order of importance, before we can presume to pour ourselves out. Circumstances oblige me to be as brief as possible for the time's quick passage demands that I bring this sermon to a close.

Just as a doctor comes to a wounded person so the Holy Spirit comes to the soul. Is it possible to find any person whom the devil's sword does not wound even after the wound of original sin has been healed by the medicine of baptism? Therefore when the Spirit draws near to a soul that says, "My wounds grow foul and fester because of my foolishness," what is the first thing the Spirit must do? Before all else he must amputate the ulcerous tumor that has grown upon the wound and prevents its healing. This ulcer, caused by inveterate bad habits, must be sliced away with the scalpel of piercing sorrow.

The pain will be bitter, but it can be alleviated with the ointment of devotion, which is nothing other than the joy born of the hope of pardon. This in turn springs from the power of self-control, from victory over sin. Soon the victor is pouring out words of thanks, "You have loosed my bonds, I will offer you the thanksgiving sacrifice."

The soul then applies the medicine of penance, a poultice of fastings, vigils, prayers and other tasks that penitents perform.

As the penitents toil they must be fed with the food of good works that they may not falter. We are not left in doubt about what the necessary food is: "My food," said Christ, "is to do the will of my Father." Hence, works motivated by love that are a sure source of strength should accompany the performance of penances. For instance it is said: "Alms is a most effective offering for all those who give in the presence of the Most High."

Food causes thirst, thus they must drink. So let the food of good works be moistened with the beverage of prayer, that a work well done may rest quietly in the stomach of conscience and give pleasure to God. In prayer we drink the wine that gladdens a person's heart, the intoxicating wine of the Spirit that drowns all memory of the pleasures of the flesh. It drenches anew the arid recesses of the conscience, stimulates digestion of the meats of good works, fills the faculties of the soul with a robust faith, a solid hope, a love that is living and true. It enriches all the actions of our life.

The sick have had their food and drink. What should they do now but take their ease and let the sweat of their labors dry while they enjoy the quiet of contemplation. Falling asleep in the midst of their prayer they dream of God. What they see is a dim reflection in a mirror, not a vision face to face. However, although it be but a vague apprehension and not an actual vision, a fleeting glimpse of the sparkling glory as it passes, utterly delicate in its impact, yet they burn with love.

Let such as these preach. Let them bear fruit. Let them show new signs and do fresh wonders. For vanity can find no toehold in those whom charity totally possesses. A total love is the law in all its fullness, it can effectively fill the heart's capacity. God himself is love and nothing created can satisfy those who are made in the image of God except the God who is love.

We need first of all compunction of heart, then fervor of spirit; thirdly, the labor of penance; fourthly, works of charity; fifthly, zeal for prayer; sixthly, leisure for contemplation; seventhly, love in all its fullness. All these are the work of the one and same Spirit.

(*On the Song of Songs* 18:5-6)

"Your name is oil poured out, therefore the maidens love you beyond measure." What does the bride mean by "beyond measure"? Greatly, vehemently, ardently. Shall I say that this spiritual doctrine may be indirectly applied to those of you who have recently arrived, as a reproof of that indiscreet zeal or rather that incredibly obstinate intemperance which we have repeatedly attempted to restrain? You have no desire to be content with the common life. The regular fast is not enough for you nor the solemn vigils nor the rules of the house nor the amount of food and clothing we have allowed you. You want to have your own private ways rather than share what is common. In the beginning you entrusted yourselves to our care, why do you take charge of yourselves again? For now you have again for master not me but that self-will by which, on the testimony of your own consciences, you have so often offended God.

It is that which urges you not to show pity for nature's needs, not to yield to reason, not to respect the advice or example of the seniors, not to obey us. Are you unaware that obedience is better than sacrifice? Have you not read in your Rule that what is done without permission of the spiritual father shall be ascribed to presumption and vainglory and not reckoned meritorious? Have you not read in the gospel the example of obedience given by the boy Jesus as a way to holiness for young people? For he had stayed behind in Jerusalem and explained that he must be busy about his Father's affairs; yet because his parents would not concur with him he did not disdain to follow them to Nazareth. So we have the Master obeying his disciples, God obeying humans, God's Word and Wisdom obeying a carpenter and his wife. And what is the comment of sacred scripture? It says, "He was subject to them." How long will you be wise in your own eyes? God entrusts himself to mortals and obeys them, and you will still walk in your own ways?

(*On the Song of Songs* 19:7)

All of us do not run with equal ardor. . . . Some are more eager for the study of wisdom, others concentrate on doing penance in the hope of pardon, others again are inspired to practice the virtues by the example of Christ's life and behavior, while yet others are roused to fervor more by the memory of his passion.

Is it possible for us to find examples of each kind?

Those ran in the fragrance of wisdom who had been sent by the Pharisees and returned to them saying, "No one ever spoke like this man!" They admired his doctrine and praised his wisdom. Nicodemus, also, was lured into running by this fragrance when he came to Jesus by night, illumined by the light of his wisdom, and went back reformed, instructed in many things.

Mary Magdalene ran in the fragrance of justice. Many sins were forgiven her because she loved much.

The tax collector ran in similar fashion. Justice himself bears witness that after he had humbly implored forgiveness for his sins, he "went home again at rights with God."

Peter ran when, after his fall, he wept bitterly to wash away his sin and be restored to righteousness. David ran when he acknowledged and confessed his crime and was privileged to be told: "The Lord has put away your sin."

Paul testifies that he ran in the fragrance of holiness when he glories in being an imitator of Christ. He said to his followers: "Take me for a model as I take Christ."

And all those were running, too, who said: "We have left everything and followed you." It was because of the desire to follow Christ that they had left all things.

A general exhortation to everyone to follow in this fragrance is contained in the words: "Those who say they abide in Christ ought to walk in the same way in which he walked."

Finally, if you wish to hear of those who ran in the fragrance of the passion, behold the martyrs.

(On the Song of Songs 22:9)

By your leave then we shall search the sacred scripture for these three things, the garden, the storeroom, the bedroom. The one who thirsts for God eagerly studies and meditates on the inspired word. Know that there we are certain to find the one for whom we thirst. Let the garden, then, represent the plain, unadorned historical sense of scripture, the storeroom its moral sense, and the bedroom the mystery of divine contemplation.

For a start, I feel my comparison of scriptural history to a garden is not unwarranted, for in it we find persons of many virtues like fruitful trees in the garden of the Bridegroom, in the paradise of God. You may gather samples of their good deeds and good habits as you would apples from trees.

(*On the Song of Songs* 23:6-9)

On this third return from Rome, my brothers, a more merciful eye has looked down from heaven. The Lion's [the anti-pope] rage has cooled, wickedness has ceased, the Church has found peace. The reprobate, the man who for almost eight years has bitterly embroiled it in schism, has been brought to nothing in its sight. But have I returned from so great dangers to be useless to you? I have been granted to your desires; I am ready to serve your advancement. Through your merits I am still alive, so I wish to live for your welfare, for your salvation.

(*On the Song of Songs* 24:1)

You are aware that a loyal companion has left me alone on the pathway of life; he who was so alert to my needs, so enterprising at work, so agreeable in his ways. Who was ever so necessary to me? Who ever loved me as he? My brother by blood, but bound to me more intimately by religious profession. Share my mourning with me, you who know these things. I was frail in body and he sustained me, faint in heart and he gave me courage, slothful and negligent and he spurred me on, forgetful and improvident and he gave me timely warning. Why was he torn from me? Why snatched from my embraces, a man of one mind with me, a man according to my heart. We loved each other in life. . . .

Our bodily companionship was equally enjoyable to both, because our dispositions were so alike. But only I am wounded by the parting. All that was pleasant we rejoiced to share, now sadness and mourning are mine alone. Anger has swept over me, rage has fastened on me. Both of us were so happy in each other's company, sharing the same experiences, talking together about them. . . .

Girard was mine, so utterly mine. Was he not mine who was a brother to me by blood, a son by religious profession, a father by his solicitude, my comrade on the spiritual highway, my bosom friend in love? And it is he who has gone from me. I feel it, the wound is deep.

(*On the Song of Songs* 26:4-9)

If we fervently persist with prayers and tears, the Bridegroom will return each time and not defraud us of our express desires. But he will return only to disappear soon again and not to return again unless he is sought for with all our heart. And so, even in this body we can often enjoy the happiness of the Bridegroom's presence. But it is a happiness that is never complete, because the joy of his visit is followed by the pain of his departure. The beloved has no choice but to endure this state until the hour when we lay down the body's weary weight and, raised aloft by the wings of desire, freely traverse the meadows of contemplation and in spirit follow the One we love without restraint wherever he goes.

(*On the Song of Songs* 32:2)

Perhaps you think that I have sullied too much the good name of knowledge, that I have cast aspersions on the learned and proscribed the study of letters. God forbid! I am not unmindful of the benefits its scholars conferred and still confer on the Church both by refuting her opponents and instructing the simple. And I have read the text: "As you have rejected knowledge so do I reject you from my priesthood" and that "the learned will shine as brightly as the vault of heaven and those who have instructed many in virtue as bright as stars for all eternity." But I recall reading too that knowledge puffs up.

All knowledge is good in itself provided it be founded on truth; but since because of the brevity of time you are in a hurry to work out your salvation in fear and trembling, take care to learn principally and primarily the doctrines on which your salvation is more intimately dependent. Do not doctors of medicine hold that the work of healing depends on a right choice in the taking of food, what to take first, what next, and the amount of each to be eaten? For although it is clear that all the foods that God has made are good, if you fail to take the right amount in due order, you obviously take them to the detriment of your health. And what I say about foods I want you to apply to the various kinds of knowledge.

It implies the order, the application and the sense of purpose with which one approaches the object of study. The order implies that we give precedence to all that aids spiritual progress; the application, that we pursue more eagerly all that strengthens love more; and the purpose, that we pursue it not through vainglory or inquisitiveness or any base motive but for the welfare of oneself or one's neighbor.

For there are some who long to know for the sole purpose of knowing and that is shameful curiosity; others who long to know in order to become known and that is shameful vanity. To such as these we may apply the words of the Satirist: "Your knowledge counts for nothing, unless your friends know you have it." There are still others who long for knowledge in order to sell its fruits for money or honors and this is shameful profiteering. Others, again, who long to know in order to be of service and this is charity. Finally, there are those who long to know in order to benefit themselves and this is prudence.

(*On the Song of Songs* 36:2-3)

Spiritual vineyards signify spiritual men within whom all things are cultivated, all things are germinating, bearing fruit and bringing forth the spirit of salvation. What was said of the kingdom of God we can equally say of these vineyards of the Lord of hosts — that they are within us. We read in the gospel that the kingdom will be given to a people who will produce its fruits. Paul enumerates these: "The fruits of the Spirit are love, joy, peace, patience, kindness, goodness, forbearance, gentleness, faithfulness, modesty, self-control, chastity." These fruits indicate our progress. They are pleasing to the Bridegroom because he takes care of us.

Do you see these novices? They came recently, they were converted recently. We cannot say of them that "our vineyard has flowered." It is flowering. What you see appear in them at the moment is the blossom. The time of fruiting has yet to come. Their new way of life, their recent adoption of a better life — these are blossoms. They have assumed a disciplined appearance, a proper deportment in their whole body. What can be seen of them is pleasing, I admit. One notices less attention to painstaking care of the body and of dress; they speak less, their faces are more cheerful, their looks more modest, their movements more correct. But since these are new beginnings, the flowers must be judged by their very novelty and as a promise of fruits rather than as the fruits themselves.

(*On the Song of Songs* 63:5-6)

Moments of Ecstasy

You ask then how I know the Word was present, when his ways can in no way be traced? He is life and power, and as soon as he enters in, he awakens my slumbering soul. He stirs and soothes and pierces my heart, for before it was hard as stone and diseased. So he has begun to pluck out and destroy, to build up and to plant, to water dry places and illumine dark ones, to open what was closed and to warm what was cold, so that my soul may bless the Lord, and all that is within me may praise his holy name.

So when the Word came to me, he never made known his coming by any signs: not by sight, not by sound, not by touch. It was not by any movement of his that I perceived his coming. Only by the movement of my heart did I perceive his presence. I knew the power of his might because my faults were put to flight and my human yearnings brought into subjection. But when he has left me, all these spiritual powers became weak and faint and began to grow cold. As often as he slips away from me, so often shall I call him back. As long as I live, the word "return," for the return of the Word, will be on my lips.

(*On the Song of Songs* 74:6f)

It is a great good to seek God. In my opinion there is no greater blessing. It is the first of gifts and the final stage of our progress. This gift is inferior to none and yields place to none. What could be superior to it, when nothing has a higher place? What could claim a higher place, when it is the consummation of all things? What virtue can be attributed to anyone who does not seek? What boundary can be set for anyone who does seek him? The psalmist says: "Seek his face always." Nor, I think, will a soul cease to seek him even when it has found him.

It is not with steps of the feet that God is sought but with the desire of the heart. When we happily find him our desire is not quenched but kindled. Does the consummation of joy bring about the consuming of desire? Rather it is oil poured upon the flames. So it is. There will be a fullness of joy, but there will be no end to desire and therefore no end to the search. Think, if you can, of this eagerness to see God as not caused by his absence, for he is always present. And think of the desire for God as without fear of failure, for grace is abundantly present.

Now see why I have begun in this way. Surely so that every soul among you who is seeking God may know that you have been forestalled and that you were found before you were seeking. This will avoid distorting your greatest good into a great evil. For this is what we do when we receive favors from God and treat his gifts as though they were ours by right not giving glory to God. Thus those who appear great because of the favors they have received are accounted as little before God because they have not given him thanks. But I am understating the case. The words I have used: "great" and "little" are inadequate to express my meaning and confuse the issue. I will make myself clear. I should have said "good" and "evil." For if a person who is very good takes the credit for his or her goodness, that one becomes correspondingly evil. For this is a very evil thing. If anyone says, "Far be it from me! I know that it is by the grace of God I am what I am, " and then seeks to take a little of the glory for the favor he or she has received, is that one not a thief and a robber? Such will hear these words: " Out of your own mouth I judge you, wicked servant." What is more wicked than for a servant to usurp the glory due the Master?

(*On the Song of Songs* 84:1f)

"I sought him whom my soul loves" — that is what you are urged to do by the goodness of him who anticipates you, who sought you, and loved you before you loved him. You would not seek him or love him unless you had first been sought and loved. Not only in one blessing have you been forestalled but in two: being loved and in being sought. For love is the reason for the search and the search is the fruit of love and its certain proof. You are loved so that you may not suppose you are sought to be punished. You are sought so that you may not complain you are loved in vain. Both these loving and manifest favors give you courage and drive away your diffidence, persuading you to return and stirring your affections. From this comes the zeal and ardor to seek him whom your soul loves, because you cannot seek unless you are sought, and when you are sought you cannot but seek.

(*On the Song of Songs* 84:5)

Happy the mind which had clothed itself in the beauty of holiness and the brightness of innocence, by which it manifests its glorious likeness, not to the world but to the Word, of whom we read that he is the brightness of eternal life, the splendor and image of the being of God.

The soul which had attained this degree now ventures to think of marriage. Why should she not, when she sees that she is like him and therefore ready for marriage? His loftiness has no terrors for her, because her likeness to him associates her with him, and her declaration of love is a betrothal. This is the form of that declaration: "I have sworn and I propose to keep your righteous judgments." The apostles followed this when they said, "See, we have left everything to follow you." There is a similar saying which, pointing to the spiritual marriage between Christ and the Church, refers to physical marriage: "For this shall a man leave his father and mother and be joined to his wife, and they two shall be one flesh." The prophet [David] says of the bride's glory: "It is good to me to cling to good, and to put my hope in the Lord." When you see a soul leaving everything and clinging to the Word with all her will and desire, living for the Word, ruling her life by the Word, conceiving by the Word what it will bring forth by him, so that she can say "for me to live is Christ and to die is gain," you know that the soul is the spouse and bride of the Word. The heart of the Bridegroom has faith in her, knowing her to be faithful, for she has rejected all things as dross to gain him. He knows her to be like him of whom it was said, "He is a chosen vessel for me." Paul's soul, indeed, was like a tender mother and a faithful wife when he said, "My little children, with whom I travail in birth again, until Christ shall be formed in you."

But notice that in spiritual marriage there are two kinds of birth and thus two kinds of offspring, though not in opposition to one another. For spiritual persons, like holy mothers, may bring souls to birth by preaching or may give birth to spiritual insights by meditation. In this latter kind of birth the soul leaves even its bodily senses and is separated from them so that in her awareness of the Word she is not aware of herself. This happens when the mind is enraptured by the unutterable sweetness of the Word, so that it withdraws or rather is transported and escapes from itself to enjoy the Word. The soul is affected in one way when it is made fruitful by the Word, in another when it enjoys the Word. In the one it is considering the needs of its neighbor, in the other it is allured by the sweetness of the Word. A mother is happy in her child, a bride is even happier in her bridegroom's embrace. The children are dear, they are pledges of his love, but his kisses give her greater pleasure. It is good to have many souls, but there is far more pleasure in going aside to be with the Word. But when does this happen and for how long? It is sweet intercourse but lasts a short time and is experienced rarely. This is what I spoke of before when I said that the final reason for the soul to seek the Word was to enjoy him in bliss.

There may be someone who will go on to ask me, "What does it mean to enjoy the Word?" I would answer that that one must find someone who has experience of it and ask that person. Do you suppose if I were granted the experience that I could describe to you what is beyond description? Listen to one who has known it: "If we are beside ourselves, it is for God; if we are in our right mind, it is for you." That is to say, it is one thing for me to be with God, and of that, God alone is the judge. It is another for me to be with you. I may have been granted this experience, but I do not speak of it. I have made allowance in what I have said, so that you could understand me. Oh, whoever is curious to know what it means to enjoy the Word, make ready your mind not your ear! The tongue does not teach this, grace does. It is hidden from the wise and prudent and revealed to children. Humility, my brothers and sisters, is a great virtue, great and sublime. It can attain to what it cannot learn, it is counted worthy to possess what it has not the power to possess. It is worthy to conceive by the Word and from the Word what it cannot itself explain in words. Why is this? Not because it deserves to do so, but because it pleases the Father of the Word, the Bridegroom of the soul, Jesus Christ our Lord, who is God above all, blessed for ever. Amen.

(On the Song of Songs 85:11)

Words of Life from a Spiritual Father

To consent is to be saved.

(Grace and Free Choice 2)

Believe me, who have experience, you will find much more laboring among the woods than you ever will among books. Woods and stones will teach you what you can never hear from any professor.

(Letters 101:2)

Sorrow for sin is indeed necessary, but it should not be an endless preoccupation. You must dwell also on the glad remembrance of God's loving kindness.

(On the Song of Songs 11:2)

If you work willingly and persevere in producing results, you will receive the reward of your labor. If you do otherwise your talent will be taken from you, but the interest will still be demanded and you will suffer the fate of a dishonest and lazy worker.

(On the Song of Songs 13:7)

If things always went wrong, no one could endure it; if they always went well, one would become arrogant.

(Letters 149:2)

How well self-discipline composes the whole bearing of a maiden's body and the temper of her mind.

(Letters 113:5)

You cannot drink from the cup of Christ and the cup of demons. The cup of demons is pride; the cup of demons is slander and envy, the cup of demons is debauchery and drunkenness, and when these fill the mind and body there is no room for Christ.

(Letters 2:10)

Easily they love more who know themselves to be loved more.

(On Loving God 7)

God not only gives me myself, he also gives me himself. In his first work he gave me myself; in his second work he gave me himself; when he gave me himself, he gave me back myself.

(*On Loving God* 15)

God is not loved without a reward, although he should be loved without regard for one.

(*On Loving God* 17)

True love is content with itself; it has its reward, the object of its love. Whatever you seem to love because of something else, you do not really love; you really love the end pursued and not that by which it is pursued.

(*On Loving God* 17)

True love merits its reward, it does not seek it.

(*On Loving God* 17)

The soul that loves God seeks no other reward than that God whom it loves.

(*On Loving God* 17)

The very law of our cupidity makes us want what we lack in place of what we have and grow weary of what we have in preference to what we lack.

(*On Loving God* 19)

The desire to experience all things is like a vicious circle, it goes on forever.

(*On Loving God* 20)

Justice is the vital, natural food of the rational soul; money can no more lessen its hunger than air can that of the body.

(*On Loving God* 21)

God makes you desire, he is what you desire.

(*On Loving God* 21)

God gave himself to merit for us, he keeps himself to be our reward.

(*On Loving God* 22)

O Lord, you are so good to the soul who seeks you, what must you be to the one who finds you?

(*On Loving God* 22)

To lose yourself, as if you no longer existed, to cease completely to experience yourself, to reduce yourself to nothing is not a human sentiment, it is a heavenly experience.

(*On Loving God* 27)

As a drop of water seems to disappear completely in a chalice of wine, taking on the wine's taste and color; as the fiery molten iron becomes so like the fire that it leaves behind its own proper form; as air filled with sunlight takes on the very clarity of the light so that it seems to be not so much lit up as to be light itself, so in the holy it is necessary that every human affection in some ineffable way will melt and flow totally into the will of God.

(*On Loving God* 28)

One can confess that the Lord is powerful, and one can confess that the Lord is good to him, and again one can confess that the Lord is simply good. The first is a slave, he fears for himself; the second is a hireling, he covets for himself; the third is a son, he honors his father. The first two seek something for themselves. Only in the son, who does not seek for himself, is found love.

(*On Loving God* 34)

Whoever is curious to know what it means to enjoy the Word, make ready your mind not your ear! The tongue does not teach this, grace does.

(*On the Song of Songs* 85:14)

Help me out of your abundance if you have it; if not, then spare yourself the trouble.

(*On the Song of Songs* 18:4)

We have received from God as part of our natural condition how to will, how to fear and how to love. In this we are creatures. But how to will the good and how to fear God and how to love God we receive with grace's touch. In this we are creatures of God.

(*Grace and Free Choice* 17)

Free will makes us our own; bad will, the devil's; and good will, God's.

(*Grace and Free Choice* 18)

The only ones who can instruct brothers and sisters are those who are merciful, those who are meek and humble.

(*The Steps of Humility and Pride* 13)

We can be as indulgent as we like for ourselves providing we remember our neighbor has the same rights.

(*On Loving God* 23)

If you are a stranger to yourself, to whom are you not? If a person is no use to himself, to whom is he useful?

(*On Consideration* 1:6)

You cannot suddenly correct every error at once or reduce excesses to moderation. There will be an opportunity at the proper time for you to pursue this little by little, according to the wisdom given by God.

(*On Consideration* 1:12)

This is exactly how the human heart behaves: what we know when it is not necessary, we forget in time of need.

(*On Consideration* 2:2)

In acquiring salvation, no one should be closer to you as a brother than the only son of your mother.

(*On Consideration* 2:6)

If you are wise, you will be content with the measure that God has apportioned you.

(*On Consideration* 2:9)

They are totally deficient who think they are in no way deficient.

(*On Consideration* 2:14)

Hold to the middle if you do not want to lose the mean.

(*On Consideration* 2:19)

Every dwelling place beyond the mean is counted an exile by the wise one.

(*On Consideration* 2:19)

Discretion is blinded by two things: anger and excessive softheartedness.

(*On Consideration* 2:20)

Those who possess, simply possess; those who love burn with zeal.

(*On Consideration* 3:9)

A stream hollows out the land where it flows; so, the flow of temporal things erodes the conscience.

(*On Consideration* 4:20)

In all things moderation is best.

(*On Consideration* 4:22)

What is above is not taught through words but is revealed through the Spirit.

(*On Consideration* 5:5)

Chronology

Note: Not all of Bernard's works can be dated with certainty. The dates given here are those the editor judges most probable.

1090   Bernard is born at Fontaines-les-Dijon in Burgundy.

1098   Robert of Molesme with his prior Alberic, subprior Stephen, and nineteen others found Citeaux, March 21.

1103   Bernard's mother Aleth dies.

1109   Alberic dies and Stephen becomes abbot of Citeaux.

1112   Bernard enters Citeaux with thirty relatives and friends.

1115   Bernard founds Clairvaux with twelve other monks.

1118   Bernard sends his first group from Clairvaux to found Trois Fontaines. By the time of Bernard's death Clairvaux would have sixty-eight filiations.
Bernard is isolated from the community for a year.

1119   Bernard's father Tescelin enters Clairvaux shortly before his death.
Pope Calixtus II confirms the *Carta Caritatis*.

1123   Bernard publishes his first work, *In Praise of the Virgin Mary*.

1124   Bernard writes *The Steps of Humility and Pride* for Godfrey of Langres, Abbot of Fontenay.

1125   Bernard writes his *Apologia* for William of St. Thierry.

1126   Cardinal Haimeric is named chancellor of the Holy Roman Church. Bernard writes *On Loving God* for him.

1128   Synod of Troyes. Bernard promotes the approbation of the Knights of the Temple and writes for them *In Praise of the New Knighthood*.
        Bernard writes *On Grace and Free Will* for William of St. Thierry.

1130   Election of Innocent II and an antipope. Bernard works eight years to heal this schism.

1131   Pope Innocent II visits Clairvaux.

1132   Bernard sent a group of monks to found Rievaulx in England.

1133   Bernard enters Rome with Innocent II. Lothar is crowned emperor.

1134   Abbot Stephen Harding of Citeaux dies.

1135   Council of Pisa. Excommunication of the antipope. Bernard begins his sermons on the Song of Songs. He would complete eighty-six sermons in this series before his death.

1137   Louis VII becomes king of France.

1138   End of the papal schism. Conrad III becomes emperor.

1139   Malachy, Archbishop of Armagh, comes to Clairvaux. Later he would return to die in his friend's arms (1148). Bernard writes his *Life of Saint Malachy*.

1140   Bernard speaks to the clerics at Paris and then writes *On the Conversion of Clerics*.

Council of Sens. Condemnation of Peter Abelard. Bernard writes *Against the Errors of Peter Abelard.*

1143 Bernard responds to two Benedictines with *On Precepts and Dispensations.*

1145 Bernard's spiritual son is elected Pope Eugene III.

1146 Bernard begins to preach the Second Crusade at Vezelay.
Bernard defends the Jews in the Rhineland.
Diet of Spires.

1147 Pope Eugene III visits Clairvaux.

1149 Bernard begins his five books *On Consideration* for Pope Eugene III.

1153 Bernard dies at Clairvaux, August 20.

1174 Bernard is canonized by Pope Alexander III, Janaury 18.

Select Bibliography

Bernard of Clairvaux. *The Works of Bernard of Clairvaux*, tr. Michael Casey et. al. (Spencer MA – Kalamazoo MI: Cistercian Publications, 1969—). *Sermons on the Song of Songs*, 4 vols.
    Sermons for the Summer Season
    Sermons on Conversion
        On Conversion to Clerics
        Lenten Sermons on the Psalm "He Who Dwells"
    Treatises, 3 vols.
        Apologia to Abbot William
        On Precept and Dispensation
        On Loving God
        The Steps of Humility and Pride
        On Grace and Free Choice
        In Praise of the New Knighthood
    Homilies in Praise of the Blessed Virgin Mary
    Parables
    The Life os Saint Malachy
    Five Books on Consideration
    The Letters of St. Bernard of Clairvaux, tr. Bruno Scott James (London: Burns and Oates, 1953).

Casey, Michael. *Athirst for God. Spiritual Desire in Bernard of Clairvaux's Sermons on the Song of Songs,* Cistercian Studies Series 77 (Kalamazoo MI: Cistercian Publications, 1987).

Cristiani, Leon. *St. Bernard of Clairvaux*, tr. M. Angeline Bouchard (Boston MA: St. Paul Editions, 1977).

Daniel-Rops, Henri. *Bernard of Clairvaux*, tr. Elizabeth Abbott (New York: Hawthorn, 1964).

Diemer, Paul. *Love Without Measure. Extracts From the Writings of St. Bernard of Clairvaux,* (Kalamazoo MI: Cistercian Publications, 1990).

Evans, G. R. *The Mind of St. Bernard of Clairvaux,* (Oxford: Clarendon Press, 1983).

Gilson, Etienne. *The Mystical Theology of Saint Bernard,* tr. A. H. C. Downes (Kalamazoo MI: Cistercian Publications, 1990).

Hufgard, M. Kilian. *Saint Bernard of Clairvaux. A Theory of Art Formulated from His Writings and Illustrated in Twelfth-Century Works of Art,* Mediaeval Studies 2 (Lewiston NY: Edwin Mellen Press, 1989).

Leclercq, Jean. *Bernard of Clairvaux and the Cistercian Spirit,* Cistercian Studies Series 16 (Kalamazoo MI: Cistercian Publications, 1975).

_____. *A Second Look at Saint Bernard,* Cistercian Studies Series 105 (Kalamazoo MI: Cistercian Publications, 1990).

_____. *Women and Saint Bernard,* Cistercian Studies Series 104 (Kalamazoo MI: Cistercian Publications, 1989).

McGuire, Brian Patrick. *The Difficult Saint: Saint Bernard and His Times,* Cistercian Studies Series (Kalamazoo MI: Cistercian Publications, 1991).

Merton, Thomas. *The Last of the Fathers,* (New York: Harcourt Brace & World, 1954). This volume includes a translation of Pope Pius XII's encyclical *Mellifluus Doctor.*

_____. *Thomas Merton on Saint Bernard,* (Kalamazoo MI: Cistercian Publications, 1980).

Pennington, M. Basil. *Last of the Fathers. The Cistercian Fathers of the Twelfth Century,* (Still River MA: St. Bede's, 1983).

_____. *Bernard of Clairvaux. A Saint's Life in Word and Image,* (Huntington IN: Our Sunday Visitor, 1994).

Pennington, M. Basil. ed., *Saint Bernard of Clairvaux. Studies Commemorating the Eighth Centenary of his Canonization,* Cistercian Studies Series 28 (Kalamazoo MI: Cistercian Publications, 1977).

Pranger, M. B. *Bernard of Clairvaux and the Shape of Monastic Thoughts: Broken Dreams,* (Leiden: Brill, 1994).

Sommerfeldt, John R. *The Spiritual Teaching of Saint Bernard,* Cistercian Studies Series 125 (Kalamazoo MI: Cistercian Publications, 1995).

William of Saint Thierry. *St. Bernard of Clairvaux,* tr. Geoffrey Webb and Adrian Walker (Westminster MD: Newman, 1960).